Discipline Without Punishment

DISCIPLINE
WITHOUT PUNISHMENT

An Account of a School

in Action

by

OSKAR SPIEL

Translated by

EDWARD FITZGERALD

Edited, with an Introduction

by

LEWIS WAY

FABER AND FABER

24 Russell Square

London

First published in mcmlxii
by Faber and Faber Limited
24 Russell Square London WC1
Printed in Great Britain by
Latimer Trend & Co Ltd Plymouth
All rights reserved

This is an abridged translation of
AM SCHALTBRETT DER ERZIEHUNG
by Oskar Spiel, originally published
in 1947 by Verlag für Jugend und Volk,
Vienna

Contents

AUTHOR'S PREFACE TO THE ENGLISH EDITION   *page* 9

INTRODUCTION BY LEWIS WAY:

    THE STORY OF THE SCHOOL   11

  I. A FIRST LOOK AT THE CLASS   17

  II. DISCIPLINE WITHOUT PUNISHMENT   31

  III. LEARNING BY THE DISCUSSION METHOD   45

  IV. ORGANIZING THE LESSONS   56

  V. SELF GOVERNMENT IN SCHOOLS   69

  VI. MONITORS, LEADERS AND HELPERS   84

  VII. THE WEEKLY DISCUSSION HOUR   97

  VIII. THE PROBLEM CHILD   114

  IX. THE CASE OF THEODORE   122

  X. THE CASE OF WILLY   130

  XI. THE CASE OF FRANK   147

  ENVOI   163

  APPENDIX: THE AUSTRIAN SYSTEM OF EDUCATION   166

  INDEX   169

7

Author's Preface

Very often people have spoken with some disdain of the actual technique of teaching. But every craftsman and artist values technical proficiency highly. No lawyer thinks it beneath his dignity to comply carefully with the formalities of his profession, and no doctor neglects to practise the tricks of his trade. Should, therefore, the teacher, with his highly responsible service to the community, be ashamed to learn the tricks of his trade and to master its technique?

There is no doubt, of course, that warmth and enthusiasm, personal value and honesty, and, above all, love, give the teaching profession its nobility, but how often and how tragically does one witness a fine and enthusiastic teacher fail in his task and lose his professional interest merely because of his ignorance of the purely technical and supposedly unimportant side of his profession.

In this book, then, I have attempted to deal with this question of technique, and to show, in particular, how Adler's system of Individual Psychology can be of service to the teacher in the practical tasks that confront him. I have proceeded more or less systematically, beginning with the simpler devices for organization and class control, with which many teachers will find themselves already familiar, and leading up to problems which need for their solution that modern understanding of the child's mind which Adler's psychology provides.

I have confined my illustrations to the relatively narrow sphere of education of boys between the ages of ten and fourteen, because my own experience as a teacher has been limited to this category. Some readers may say: 'Good: Granted that Adler's Individual Psychology is applicable to the education of boys between the ages of ten and fourteen, what about the education of younger children? Children between the ages of six and ten? Youths? Girls?' To this I would answer: 'One would not, of course, speak to a six-year-old child in the same way as to a child of twelve. The form will naturally vary. But it will always and in all circumstances be a question of educating in the spirit of Individual Psychology. It is for followers of Individual Psychology who are kindergarten or elementary teachers, or who work in institutions or children's homes or as scoutmasters, to show how—with the necessary adaptations to changed circumstances—the methods I describe remain applicable.'

I have considered also whether the argument advanced in this book could in any way be invalidated by the differences between the Austrian and the English systems of education. I believe such differences to be unimportant from the point of view here taken, and that the suggestions I have put forward are perfectly applicable under either system. But for the sake of the teacher who would like to compare the educational system known to him with that under which the work I describe has been done, I have placed a short summary of the present Austrian system as an Appendix.

OSKAR SPIEL

The Story of the School

W hen the First World War ended with the collapse of the Austro-Hungarian Empire and the overthrow of the Hapsburg Monarchy a young teacher, such as Spiel then was, felt himself faced by a dilemma. The Hapsburg Monarchy had imposed upon the children of Austria a rigidly authoritarian, semi-militaristic form of education. Obedience and learning by heart were the prime objectives. Such could not be the objectives in the new, democratic society which was then shaping. How, the young Spiel asked himself, could a form of education be devised that would fit the child to take his place as a responsible citizen in this new democracy?

It was a time of famine and inflation. The war and the revolution had broken up homes, and the Vienna streets were filled with abandoned and vagabond children. As happens after every great war, the problem of juvenile delinquency had become acute. The city authorities had sought to cope with this problem by the formation of Child Guidance Clinics, and they had appointed the psychologist Alfred Adler to take charge of the majority of them. It was a bold step, for the methods of modern psychology were then entirely novel.

To run his clinics—thirty in all, dispersed in all the districts of the city—Adler organized a body of voluntary workers. But many of these workers were still insufficiently trained in his new principles and there was urgent need to recruit still others. Lectures, which he gave them untiringly, were not enough. There had also to be practical demonstrations. Adler therefore began the practice of admitting students while he was conducting the analysis of a child. Of course, cries were heard from opponents that he was thus 'violating the sanctity of the consulting room'. Perhaps he was, but the need for more trained workers was pressing, and it was also found that the children seemed to benefit in the most surprising fashion. Often Adler would turn from the child he was analysing to the audience and ask one or other of its members if he had not experienced similar difficulties as the child when he was young. A discussion would then develop, and the child, who had hitherto experienced himself only as the object of adult disapproval, would find himself instead the centre of a sympathetic and understanding group, some of whom confessed that they had known just as bad failures as he, that these were not a reason for worry or guilt, and that they could be overcome. Thus, almost accidentally, out of the urgent need to train students, was born the method of group-therapy, which has been extended in our day to adult groups and is being practised on an ever-widening scale.

'I had, of course, often heard in Vienna of Adler's Child Guidance Clinics,' Spiel remembers, 'but I had hitherto supposed that his psychology could only be of help in directly abnormal cases. I had not realized the universal value of Adler's teachings or that they could be applied to every child by every teacher.' Spiel was, however, sufficiently interested in these new psychological theories to attend a Congress of Individual Psychology, where he heard Adler expound his views personally for the first time. 'I had previously studied Freud's psychology for a year,' he says, 'but I could not find there anything that I could apply to my work as a teacher. But this Berlin Congress was a revelation to me. The moment I heard Adler's opening lecture I realized that I had found the key to my difficulties.'

Spiel had seen that Adler's method was the answer to his question —how to educate children to take their place in a democratic society. Still today, in so far as we rely upon punishment and authority in our schools, this answer has not been learned, and our educational methods remain incompatible with our ideals. Spiel had also seized the point that if a school class were to be led upon the same lines as Adler practised in dealing with an individual child, this class would take on the character of a therapeutic group—a group that could be used to help the backward, stimulate the lazy and quiet the rebel. It solved the problem of discipline. At the same time it fulfilled the dream of every true educator, that of making the school not merely a place of instruction but of character training. Under Spiel, a class becomes an object lesson in the art of democratic and co-operative living-together.

With his brilliant colleague, the late Professor Birnbaum, Spiel spent the four years from 1920 to 1924 in an intensive study of the work of Adler's Child Guidance Clinics. They had many problems to work out together, especially the problem of how to transfer the technique of treating one child to the treatment of a collective. They had to devise a system of class discussion to replace the ordinary instructional lesson given by the teacher and to find ways of meeting the many formidable difficulties of discipline which this system raised. Fortunately, at that time, education was in process of being liberalized. In 1926, the Social Democratic régime had instituted reforms which swept away the old authoritarian methods in favour under the Hapsburg Monarchy. The pupils were no longer expected to sit passively and imbibe instruction. Instead, they were encouraged to find out things for themselves, to ask their own questions and to manage their own affairs. This 'active' method, as it might be called, whose potentialities and limitations are discussed by Spiel in his third chapter, made a suitable basis for the introduction of Individual Psychology. The educational authorities were also in a state of mind to be interested in new experiments, and the President of the Viennese Board of Education, Glockel, paid many visits to see the classes which Spiel was conducting. Finally, in 1931, through Glockel's influence, permission was obtained for the launching of a complete 'Individual Psychology Experimental School' in the 20th District of Vienna.

The school thus started by Spiel and Birnbaum, and of which the present book is a record, was a secondary school for boys, aged ten to fourteen, in every respect similar to the other secondary schools which are under the direction of the Vienna City Council. Spiel was required to conform to the curricula set for all the other schools and to maintain the scholastic standards demanded by the educational authorities. He was not in a position to sacrifice standards in set subjects for the sake of concentrating on some higher educational aim, nor was he free to indulge in the sort of experimentation which might be possible under a private foundation. His methods, therefore, cannot be said to depend for their success upon the backing of special circumstances or special prerogatives not open to the ordinary teacher.

In point of fact, the school laboured under special disadvantages. Being situated in one of the most impoverished districts of Vienna, the children who attended it came from poor and ignorant homes. In 1931, also, the world economic depression, which had set in two years previously, was having its worst effects and there was mass unemployment in Vienna. Dr. Madeleine Ganz, in her study of Spiel's work already published in this country,[1] has given a description of the conditions which I cannot do better than quote: 'The children often arrived at school in lamentable condition. On many occasions, in the depth of winter, we have seen them hungry and shivering with cold. The school itself was very badly heated, for it lacked the money to procure a sufficiency of fuel—some classrooms were occupied until six in the evening, yet the heat was turned off at ten in the morning. For this reason, the opening of windows in winter time was not allowed during the recreation periods, even though these had to be spent in class for lack of a courtyard or open-air playground. These deplorable conditions cannot fail to have made their depressing influence felt throughout the schooling of these necessitous children. If such a school, then, manages to give positive results, if it can already claim many successes, they cannot be attributed to external conditions particularly appropriate to children's needs.'

The economic crisis of those years was followed by the resurgence of authoritarian régimes which looked unfavourably upon educational experiments. The Child Guidance Clinics attached to the State schools, which Adler and his co-workers had run so successfully, were suppressed for these political reasons, and in February 1934 came the end also of Spiel's Experimental School. It was only after eleven years of Fascism and war that, in September 1946, Spiel obtained permission to reopen. Again, this was a lean and hungry time in the affairs of Austria. In the beginning, Spiel tells us, 'the two Higher Elementary Schools which formed the basis of the planned Experimental School were housed in a provisional building. It was a rather derelict house with cardboard for windows and no heat. We suffered bitterly from the cold, and all were hungry, children as well as teachers. The teachers were sceptical, struggling for their mere existence, and yet were somehow ready to take up the struggle for the souls of these miserable, neglected children. Some of the old teachers remained at the school where they had served during the Fascist era, others came from various schools, whom we had invited to co-operate, some were driven by an inner impulse to join the new school. The greatest drawback was that they had not the least knowledge of Individual Psychology.'

In 1947, conditions were improved. The school was moved into

[1] M. Ganz: *The Psychology of Alfred Adler and the Development of the Child* (Routledge).

14

another building and an Elementary School was added. The three schools were now composed of 10 elementary school classes, 16 higher elementary and 3 one-year classes for children over fourteen —a total of 29 classes, comprising 1,100 children and a staff of 44 teachers. The pupils of this school—an unusually large one for Vienna—are still drawn almost entirely from the poorest part of the population. Thirty-eight per cent of the children come from proletarian flats consisting of only one room and a kitchen, another 38 per cent live in flats with one big and one small room and a kitchen, and only 2·8 per cent can boast of a bathroom. The parents are mostly railway and tram employees, skilled or semi-skilled workers or poor tradesmen.

A particular problem which Spiel has had to face has been that as his reputation for dealing with 'difficult' children increases so he becomes more and more pressed to accept into his school children from far outside his own Vienna district, children who have been expelled from one school after another, who have been stealing, who have committed sexual offences, or who have been caught by the police as vagabonds. Every teacher knows how upsetting it is to introduce such problem children into a normal class. Yet Spiel is able to report: 'Of the 63 children with clinical records whom the police or the social workers sent to our school in 1952–3, 60 were kept and restored to normality. Three had to be turned away because they were endangering the other children and were sent to special institutions.'

To some teachers who read this book it may seem that to carry out Spiel's suggestions would require of them a knowledge of psychological principles which is outside their scope as teachers. Especially, they may object that it is not their function to undertake the psychotherapy of the problem child, and that such a child should properly be sent to a Guidance Clinic. This is a viewpoint that must command everyone's sympathy, and it is not to be supposed that the teacher who comes upon the method of Individual Psychology for the first time is in a position to deal with the more difficult cases cited by Spiel in his three final chapters. The description of these cases nevertheless forms an illuminating illustration of the general method of dealing with children which Individual Psychology recommends. It points the way to what the teacher can or could do once he has gained the necessary practical experience of the method. Individual Psychology is not so specialized a science as to be unapproachable by the layman. On the contrary, it was presented by Adler deliberately in such a way as to become of maximum service to the teacher in his profession, and it was his principal hope that it would be so used. 'We need the most intimate co-operation between the psychiatrist and the teacher,' he wrote. 'The teacher must know everything that the psychiatrist knows, so that after discussing the child's problem he can proceed on his own without further help.'[1] That this is by no means an unrealizable ideal is well shown by the present book.

LEWIS WAY

[1] *What Life Should Mean to You*, p. 159.

CHAPTER I

A First Look at the Class

Let us enter the class. Heads down and writing away at some task sit thirty-six boys. Their average age is ten. The classroom is quiet. Slowly one of the boys raises his head and looks round at his neighbour as though seeking help. No sooner has he started his work than he is overcome by a feeling of anxiety and helplessness. You can see in his eyes the fear that he will be unable to perform his task. It is a fear which characterizes his whole nature; prevents him from co-operating freely in the discussions of his fellows: makes him hang back in the playground instead of taking his part in the games; finds expression in his dreams; wakes him up screaming in the night, pale and trembling, and robs his mother of her precious sleep to console and soothe him. He is the nervous type, frightened of everything; and life to him is like a threatening dragon to be passed anxiously on tiptoe or fled from with trembling knees.

What a different type his neighbour is! He doesn't tremble when he has to stand in front of the class and say his piece. He speaks calmly and confidently. Nevertheless, he is definitely an introvert. He is a silent child, and he does not often take part in the noisy games of his fellows. He prefers to stand to one side and watch. He seeks no friends and he has none. He goes his own way; withdraws into his loneliness, and builds up his own world, separated by an invisible wall from the rushing, tossing stream of life around him.

The youngster with the smooth girlish face and the dark liquid eyes which look out, lost in thought, on to the world, lives in a different sphere again. For him all the fairy tales told by his mother, a quiet and delicate woman, are still reality. A plot of grass in the park is a fairy sward where gnomes get up to their tricks and elves still dance a ring of roses. With his bricks he builds up palaces of marble, gold and ivory, and there he enters as a fairy prince, and at his side is the fairy princess he has rescued from a thousand dangers. He is a little intimidated by the harsh world of reality with its sums—sums which, according to his wicked teacher, can be done only in two ways: rightly or wrongly. It is a world in which there are very few playmates ready to wander with him in the realm of fantasy, ready to be his companion in his dreams. What else can he do but long himself back out of this harsh world into another, but fast-fading, world where his day dreams revolve around his longing?

But the boy behind him is of different metal. He is quite at home in the workaday world. Look at the way he stretches himself and yawns out loud. You can almost read his thoughts: 'School work isn't exactly fun, but it's not too bad either. You've only got to look after yourself. Why write four pages when two will do? After all, what can the old boy do? One wigging or a bad mark more or less doesn't really matter. When it keeps on raining you get used to the sound of the drops until in the end you don't hear them at all. And, after all, the old boy pays more attention to me than he does to the swots. So why should I bother to look at the blackboard when he's explaining something? And as for doing anything on my own—what an idea! It's much easier and much less trouble to copy from my neighbour. "Buck up! Buck up!" he's always saying. But why should I? It's not as though I couldn't do it perfectly well if I wanted to. He's always calling me a lazybones and telling me to think of the future. Let him worry about it; why should *I*? It'll be all right when the time comes. Why should I exert myself when I can take it easy? It's very nice to stroll through life and know at the same time that if you liked to put your back into it you could make the others sit up.'

And you surely know that delicate pale-faced boy over there? I expect he has often made you despair, too. Let me introduce him: our tearful Tommy. What a hard life he leads here amongst his fellows! And how hard he makes it for them—and for the teacher, too! Where's he's concerned every word must be carefully weighed before it's spoken. He's got a very fine ear for the slightest suggestion of reproach. Be careful how you touch him in play, because a pat for him is like a blow for others. And then there's that wicked boy who takes a delight in making fun of him so that he bursts into tears and runs off to tell the teacher! What can Tearful Tommy do but anxiously avoid anything which might threaten pain, danger or defeat?

A First Look at the Class

But all his efforts are in vain when there's a boy in the class who never misses an opportunity of tripping up others in order to shine himself. All the other boys have reason to know his strength, and every day he gets to work on the punching-ball. The little ruffian knows how to arrange his victories. He provokes his victim with hurtful and mocking words, with aggressive stares and challenging gestures. His wounding chaff and insults are soon followed by apparently playful pushing and shoving, until the victim, provoked beyond endurance, hits out. That is what the young scamp has been waiting for, and now he goes for his victim with flailing fists until he has him on the floor, defeated. The last ounce is then squeezed out of his victory; the victim is mercilessly mocked; and the exact technique by which he was defeated is explained boastfully to the onlookers. And his toadies applaud his prowess, outdo each other in flattering words for his strength and his skill, and make up to him obsequiously for fear that they may be his next victims and in the secret hope that they may protect themselves by winning his friendship.

There is only one other boy in the class the young ruffian fears, and to him he plays second fiddle. This is the born gang leader. He doesn't come into the foreground very much, but he is all the more active unseen. He rules over a certain circle of children, and they are his willing followers. His leadership does not depend on brute force, but on his knowledge of embarrassing situations and misdeeds, on the exploitation of antagonisms, on the pushing forward of certain chosen middlemen, and on a cunning technique of blackmail. He rules them by his personality and he is the centre of many exaggerated stories. Tremendous deeds which impress the others are invented around him, and he is invested with a cloak of mystery. The boys he pushes forward bask in his reflected glory and they share in the fruits of his success. His subjects are fascinated by the mystery which surrounds him, and it produces a submission amounting almost to bondage, a submission prepared to pay any tribute demanded. They are ready even to surrender their own egos and to take part in things which go against the grain of their inner conviction.

The saucy boy is a much more likeable type. He is always in the centre of attention amongst his fellows. Sometimes the atmosphere in class resembles that of a race meeting. Bets are actually made as to what he will dare to do today. And if the saucy fellow should happen to become so interested in his work that an hour passes without his having delivered one of his notoriously impudent remarks, then there is great disappointment, and regretfully the word goes round: 'What a pity! He couldn't pluck up enough courage today.' When he hears that the saucy boy is cut to the quick. He can't let them say that about him. And during the next lesson he begins his impudent performance anew. For everything the teacher says he's got an answer. He pulls faces. He spots his opponent's weakest point and pounces on it at once with stinging mockery. He doesn't mind having to pay for his performance. Even when he gets a punishment there's always some quip ready to hoist the banner of victory even in defeat. Outwardly the other boys pretend to be shocked at his impudence, but inwardly they are hugging themselves with glee. The saucy boy is the hero of the class. His audience applauds: 'He's a lad. He's not afraid of anything.' The audience is so grateful to anyone who makes a change and brings a bit of amusement into its life.

Although the types we have mentioned so far may not all be found in every classroom, the joker is probably there. His inventive wit is inexhaustible. His features are capable of the most improbable distortion and his limbs make the most grotesque movements. He imitates a clown, a favourite figure for all children. Deftly he attaches a notice to another boy's back: 'What's the joke?' He puts the wastepaper basket over his head during the lesson and grins at the class through the wickerwork to raise a laugh. His mere appearance is the signal for merriment. A few grimaces and there is a storm of laughter overwhelming any appeal to seriousness in class; and even when it has finally subsided there are still stifled chuckles for a while until order is finally restored. The joker is the centre point of interest, and that flatters him. His class-mates laugh at his antics, applaud him, admire him. He is certain of the unfailing sympathy of the whole class—and even the teacher finds it difficult to be really angry with him; too often he has to laugh himself at the usually harmless but comic antics of the boy.

What may be called the 'common burr' is a much greater nuisance. He ceaselessly dances attendance on the teacher, and keeps asking the most pointless questions merely in order to attract notice. He is at the teacher's side at every possible opportunity, offering all sorts of unwanted services: 'May I?', 'Shall I?', 'Please let me', 'Can I?' His questions, his wants and his complaints fasten themselves on to the teacher like the tentacles of an octopus—as soon as one is cast off the other attaches itself. The teacher is given no peace, and the unwanted attentions can even encroach upon his private life.

20

Need we introduce to you any more types? You certainly already know them from your own wide experience as a teacher: the ninny, the flatterer, the bungler, the whiner, the sensation-monger, the windbag, the disturber, the fusspot, the boaster, the tell-tale, the truant, the 'difficult' ones, the 'awkward' ones, the defiant ones. There are a thousand different ways in which defects of character development show themselves, and if they persist into the world outside they lead to restrictions, interruptions and disturbances, even tragedies, in adult social life.

There would be cause for despair indeed if there were not also other and very different types amongst our school children. There is the real leader, for example. His chief characteristic is his ability. He fascinates the other children by his personality and they cling to him with all their youthful loyalty. He is intelligent enough to grasp a given situation quickly and to adapt himself to it. His fantasy is lively and he is constantly inventing new ideas to bind the other children to him. He is serious, but he can be cheerful at the right moment. He leads a group of children around him, but he leads them with a creative initiative that develops community values. His conciliatory character makes it easy for him to resolve antagonisms and reconcile opposing opinions, and he carries out his mediatory activity, encouraging others to positive action, without any fuss or ostentation. The success of his activity wins him the respect, the admiration, even the devotion of the other children.

A related type is the leader in a particular sphere. His special form of unifying activity is usually confined to one field. Otherwise not particularly prominent, he is perhaps a popular games leader. In games his leadership is not only undisputed but willingly, even gladly, accepted and acknowledged. His inventiveness in producing variations is inexhaustible, and he apportions the roles with a confidence which impresses all the others and always leaves him automatically leader. Or such a type is supreme, say, in some manual activity, perhaps bookbinding, and on account of his skill he holds a special and often envied position amongst his fellows. Such specialist leader types are to be met with in various spheres and they are very welcome adjuncts to the work of the teacher.

Another very valuable type is what might be described as 'the helper'. The helper is not particularly interested 'in influencing and organizing the others; he is not in direct and close contact with the others in the way leaders are'. 'Generally speaking this type is to be

21

met with amongst children who are well liked on account of their favourable position amongst their fellows but who, on account of a lack of social activity, are never in the centre of class life. Apparently their relationship with the others in the typical function of helpers is primarily guided by objective reasons. The help they give is not confined to certain definite children, their friends for example, but offered as and where it is required. Their own pleasure in giving help seems to be the chief factor at work.'[1] The helper is an agreeable and welcome type.

Thus every class is essentially made up of opposing tendencies, and the teacher stands in the middle of it all. Throughout the whole of his exacting activity he is conscious of how difficult it is to prevent these various conflicting forces from breaking up altogether, to reconcile opposing tendencies, and intervene fruitfully at the right place. And all this has to be achieved merely in order to make instruction possible at all. No outsider, no father, no mother and no school inspector is in a position to grasp the whole difficulty of amalgamating these very heterogenous elements. Only the teacher, who has to deal with all these various types day after day, and whose task it is—not imposed upon him by anyone else but arising from the nature of things—to guide the children to reasonably harmonious collaboration in the work of the school, can realize its whole difficulty; it is only he who feels its urgency at first hand.

Thus it is understandable that the demand for suitable means of education, or re-education, comes first from the teacher himself. Teachers cannot content themselves with merely observing the psychological manifestations of children and then retiring quietly to their studies to work out ingenious theories. It is not much use to them that the similarity of so many cases makes it possible to classify children according to types. For teachers each lesson is a demand for immediate practical action.

The situation of the teacher is made still more difficult by the attitude of many of the parents, most of whom regard the school as nothing but a place in which instruction is given, and whose interest is therefore confined to their children's academic progress. Others again regard school as a necessary evil and are therefore inclined to consider everything beyond the bare necessities as superfluous, and to reject it on the grounds that 'in practical life' there is no room for

---

[1] Karl Reininger in *Praxis und Theorie der Schulklasse*, issued by Burger and Stejskal, Deutscher Verlag fur Jugend und Volk, Vienna, p. 213.

any such trifling. In still other cases, apparently enthusiastic approval for the measures adopted by a teacher turns out to be merely a cloak for bitter opposition. And then there is the type of parent who is over-anxious and over-zealous in his or her desire to protect the children, and who regards any deviation from his own pet methods as a personal insult. And which of us has not met the parent who is always prepared to help the teacher with a contribution from his own vast fund of educational theories? We are faced with parents as the propagandists of a thousand and one forms of contradictory educational methods. Their slogans resound in our ears in unholy confusion. 'Children must learn to express their own personalities.' 'Children must learn to subordinate themselves.' 'Spare the rod and spoil the child.' 'Love is all that's necessary.' 'My child must have things better than I did.' 'Just let them grow up; things come right of themselves in the end.'

And the depressing thing is that all these various views of education, from mollycoddling and pampering to nagging and harsh treatment, have themselves been formed on the basis of certain life styles, themselves the result of harmful educational traditions or of a struggle against them. The kind of education approved by the parents is always the expression of certain definite views on life. There can be no doubt that all these views represent real inner convictions; their holders mean well, and whatever they do is done with the best intentions. They are acting in perfect sincerity. In spite of this, however, how often do they come to us, confused and helpless, and with a touching confidence that the expert will put them right. 'What am I to do, teacher? I've tried everything: kindness and severity. But it's all no use.'

Well, what is to be done?

The workaday world which awaits the children outside the school is a hard one. It demands capable men and women. The school must therefore find ways and means of making the children entrusted to it able to stand up to the onerous demands which will subsequently be placed on them. That is why schools try to sort out the talented. The underlying cause of this search for talent amongst the children is the belief that the individual child must be specifically prepared for the existing labour market. It explains the present tendency towards experimental psychology and the great interest in tests to reveal the children's abilities and peculiarities. Schools are therefore inclined to support psychological systems whose attention is primarily directed to the qualities a child possesses, systems that Adler has dubbed 'possession psychologies'.

Thus human society in its present-day economic pattern regards the school primarily as a place of instruction in various subjects and skills, and those whom society has appointed to attend to these matters lay chief stress on the level of performance attained by school children who are subsequently to be launched into a highly commercialized society. This attitude then largely determines the aims of instruction and the fixing of the curricula; and school authorities pay chief attention to the tangible successes obtained by a teacher in his special subject or subjects. This is quite readily understandable because during his short visits a school inspector can hardly observe the *educational* efforts of the teacher adequately, and still less can he recognize the educational success of the teacher in respect of individual children. All the inspector can do is to examine the easily discoverable performance levels of the children and pass an expert judgement on the methods of teaching employed. When we consider that in addition the school inspector is burdened by a great volume of administrative matters, then it is easy to see that the educational work of the teacher, subject to the administrative activity of the authorities above him, is itself in danger of being forced into bureaucratic channels.

If a teacher, impelled by his educational vocation, feels it necessary to stress the properly educational side of his activities to a greater extent than before, then for him the urge from above for 'visible results', for tangible and measurable successes, represents a very serious hindrance. At the same time, he has been appointed a teacher by those whom society has entrusted with the control of its educational system, and he finds it impossible to shake off this outside pressure altogether despite the fact that, in the midst of all the everyday problems of the school itself, he may well recognize that *even the so urgently demanded instructional successes depend primarily on the correct attitude of the children to life and to the tasks it involves.*

Our work as teachers has been made more difficult, even been upset, by the children who are always late for school, who never have their things ready, who play truant, and so on. As teachers we are only too well aware of all these things because they make our lives difficult. Of course, we have done our best to remedy them, and we have all had resort to the usual recipes and remedies. Let us take a look at some of these:

24

A First Look at the Class

(1) *Exhortation.* How many thousand of times have we said: 'John, pay attention!' 'Richard, look at the blackboard!' 'Albert, stop playing with things!'? How many times have we remonstrated with children and tried to guide them in the right direction by exhortation. And with what result? Only in very rare cases do we find that such exhortations prove effective. Generally speaking they have to be repeated again and again. Now why does this obvious method of dealing with inattention prove so fruitless? Whoever has once gained an insight into the way the human mind work knows the answer. Exhortation does not touch the fundamental attitude of the child, and it is this attitude that is making the child seek to evade co-operation.

Let us take a minor example: Edward is not paying attention again. He is rummaging around in his school satchel. He is called to order. For the moment that may have some effect, but it will hardly be effective in the long run. Now let us look at the situation from Edward's viewpoint. He happens to notice a book lying on his desk or his form. As he doesn't require it for the moment he thinks to himself: 'I'll put that away and be tidy, like they're always telling me.' And the long and detailed process of putting it away in his satchel begins. In the middle of it comes the teacher's reproof. Now Edward can kill two birds with one stone. First of all, whilst he was putting his book away his attention was withdrawn from the teacher, and that is his secret aim, and secondly, seen from his own viewpoint, he can now think: 'Teacher's reproof was an injustice, because I was only being tidy like he's always telling me. If I hadn't been good I wouldn't have cleared up.' How wonderful! Edward is able to withdraw his attention with a good conscience! The teacher's reproof refers to the lack of attention, but Edward's mind is engaged with the problem of tidiness. Thus teacher and child are on two different planes, and in the end the personal attitude of the child remains untouched by the teacher's efforts at reform.

The way children receive reproofs and exhortations can be seen from the excuses they make to their parents: 'Teacher told me off for lack of attention, but I had to do up my shoelace.' 'I was looking for the book the boy next to me had borrowed and he made such faces.' And so on. Such excuses are quite serious from the child's viewpoint. That is how they see the thing. They feel themselves innocent. In their eyes, persons and things that hinder them from being attentive are at fault. Only very rarely does a child see that he was at fault,

25

that his own attitude was wrong, and then recognize the justice of the teacher's reproof.

It would be a very easy matter to quote many similar examples to demonstrate the inadequacy of the exhortation method, perhaps even its uselessness in cases, shall we say, of truancy, late-coming, untidiness and so on. But it would not be worth while. Whoever has acquainted himself with the way the human mind works realizes that it is no use trying to achieve temporary results by exhortation, and that instead other educational methods must be used, methods which reach the fundamental attitude of the child and therefore hold out some hope of changing it.

2. *Threats*. In all probability no educational method is used more often in school than this. It would be a waste of time for us to enumerate all the things that are threatened. The end result is almost invariably the same: the degree of childish wrong-doing is curbed—although even that minor success is not always attained. The fact that the teacher adopts such a method again and again is itself a proof that in the last resort nothing has changed in the structure of the childish character. Of course, there is no doubt that vehement threats can intimidate a child, but then it will not react by changing its attitude, but only by making some tactical change.

Charles, for example, was a good and ambitious pupil. He was always first in the class and he distinguished himself by especial zeal. Then another pupil came into the class from another school, and before long it was seen that the newcomer was ahead of Charles in mathematics. Bitter rivalry opened up between the two. One day there was an examination in mathematics and Charles failed. It turned out that he had played truant on examination day. The teacher threatened him with expulsion: 'We don't want truants in the school. If you do that again you will be expelled.' This threat, probably not uttered in all seriousness, had the effect of intimidating Charles. Never again did he play truant. But he gave up trying. At the same time he knew how to keep up appearances. When his schoolfellows pointed out that his rival was ahead of him he would reply, 'Oh, him! Anything he can do I can do ten times better. But I don't bother with homework. Do you think I'd swot all day long like he does! Not likely! But if I wanted to. . . .' Charles had taken refuge in the symptom: laziness. He still practised evasion, but in a different form. He had made a symptomatic change, that was all. His funda-

26

mental attitude had remained the same: flight from a task he thought would prove too difficult for him.

Now is it really satisfactory from the educational point of view to bring about a change merely in the symptoms? The effect of threats depends entirely on the child's life-style. With mollycoddled children threats can produce pathological disturbances with all sorts of spiritual and physical reactions. For instance, threats may easily strengthen a contact—with a mother, for example—which hinders the solution of the life problems the child is called upon to solve, with the result that the child's fundamental attitude is reinforced. In other words, threats bring about exactly the contrary of what is aimed at. Where a child has been brought up lovelessly and has therefore adopted a belligerent attitude, threats will strengthen his attitude, because the threats will only confirm the child in his belief that he is surrounded on all sides by enemies and that his defensive belligerency is the right way to behave. The manner in which a child has come to regard life, the particular attitude which he has taken up towards it, is effective against all threats. It is not enough to bring about temporary improvement in outward conduct by means of threats. The only lasting improvement is to bring about a change in the fundamental attitude of the child.

3. *Punishment*. There are teachers who cannot imagine how a class can run smoothly without punishments. We are well aware that we are touching on a very delicate point here. The system of Individual Psychology has perhaps done more than anything else to curb the demand put forward by enthusiasts that punishment in school should be abolished at once, a fact that the author can vouch for from personal experience. The system of Individual Psychology approaches the educational problem much too seriously and practically for it to demand that the authorities should officially prohibit punishment in schools. Whoever looks at the position soberly and without excessive idealism is well aware that the mere abolition of punishment in the schools could only have one certain result: chaos. It is not accidental that wherever punishment was radically abolished the result was miserable failure, so much so, that the old system had to be reintroduced. This was the logical end of the Utopian idea that it is quite enough to surround the problem child with love, whereupon everything will come right. Ferdinand Birnbaum hit the nail on the head when he declared: 'A child who makes difficulties, suffers from difficulties.' The psyche of such a child is under a strain. 'The healing

27

power of love does not produce relaxation in a psyche under strain. The healing process is much more difficult. Otherwise it would be sufficient to surround every problem child with love and then he would be cured.'[1]

Thus the task before us is not to replace punishment by a too-gushing love, but—and this is the belief of Individual Psychology—to replace punishment gradually by the use of other and more effective methods of education. And the stress here must be laid on the word 'gradually'. Education without punishment can only be an aim. Just as long as the teacher cannot command, and has no practice in, more effective methods of education he cannot get along without punishment. However, we regard it as imperative that teachers should make it their business to learn and practise these more effective methods.

In order that there shall be no possibility of misunderstanding on this decisive point let us make the position quite clear by a parallel: When a doctor is called to a child suffering from diphtheria he invariably finds the mother particularly anxious because the child's temperature is so high, and he will then probably say more or less the following: 'Don't worry about the fever; that is only an external symptom. The real trouble behind the fever is diphtheria and I shall deal with that by injecting a serum.' Thus the doctor will draw a clear dividing line between the symptom and the sickness which produces the symptom. Something similar is necessary in education. Fear, defiance, bad temper, aggressiveness, truancy, laziness, untruthfulness and so on are all merely external symptoms. Knowledge of the human mind has shown us that behind these symptoms there lies, as the real sickness, a lack of community feeling and discouragement. Whoever sees only the sympton and tries to drive it out of a child by punishment is doing the same sort of thing as a doctor would be doing who gave a child suffering from diphtheria quinine to lower its temperature rather than an injection of serum to deal with the diphtheria itself.

Now when the teacher who follows the methods of Individual Psychology opposes the use of punishment he is justified in doing so because he has educational methods at his disposal which are far more effective and which deal not with the external symptoms but with the fundamental and erroneous attitude of the child towards life. In other words, Individual Psychology does not merely deprive

[1] Jahn-Adler, *Religion und Individualpsychologie*, p. 89.

28

the severe teacher of his educational methods and then leave him to his fate, but it gives him other and more effective methods, methods that not only make educational work really possible in the first place, but also make it easier.

The point at issue is this: Individual Psychology teaches us that in the last resort every punishable action committed by a child can be understood from his individual life-style. The urge of the child towards superiority leads him often into erroneous judgements upon the world about him and into taking up an erroneous attitude towards it. This brings him into conflict with situations which can be fundamentally resolved only by the removal of the error and the breaking down of the attitude founded upon it. Later on we shall deal in some detail with situations which call for punishment, and therefore these general indications will serve for the moment.

4. _Rewards_. The characteristic feature of this educational method is that it relates to a person rather than to a performance. For example, it is one thing to say to a child: 'This drawing does everything which is required of it,' and quite another to say: 'Because you have done this drawing so well you can go to the theatre today.' In the first case we speak of the performance, and in the second place we speak of the child himself. To recognize the quality of a performance is a different thing from rewarding a person. Whoever has once recognized that the value of a human being lies not in his person but in his doings, his performance, will realize at once where the danger of the method lies. A reward changes the object of the effort. A child no longer works for the thing itself, but for the reward which follows it. He no longer takes up an objective attitude, but a personal one. He no longer makes a proper drawing because he realizes that it is useless unless it is done properly, but in order to enhance his own personality. He no longer plays fair with his fellows because that is the only right thing to do, but because he expects to be rewarded for his fair play. No educational method does more to turn the objectively justifiable striving for perfection into a striving for superiority than does the system of rewards.

If anyone now feels inclined to take us up on a question of principle, and asks: 'So we're not to give children tickets for the theatre?' we reply: 'Of course we should give children tickets for the theatre!' But it is a very different thing when someone says: 'I am going to give you a ticket for the theatre today because you did your lesson so well,' instead of saying: 'I thought you would like to go to the theatre today and so I am giving you a ticket.' The first is giving the child a reward, the second is just giving it a pleasure.

We therefore regard the effect of these educational methods—rewards, punishments, threats, exhortation and others we could name—as very limited. We shall seek rather, with the insight which we have won by our observation and our interpretation of the erroneous aims of the child to bring him to greater self-realization, to reveal his fundamental errors and to show him how his wrong attitude has developed. Only this self-realization can persuade him to take off the distorting glasses through which he has been looking at the world and adopt a new attitude to the tasks of life.

The teacher will also adopt various ways and means to strengthen the courage of the difficult child and to assist him to take his place in the community and make his contribution towards it. This certainly cannot be brought about merely by comforting words. The child must be brought to enjoy the first flush of success on the useful side of life, and the teacher must previously arrange the circumstances in such a fashion that any experiences of success will come about apparently naturally. At the same time the favourable forces developed in the child by this encouragement and by the new aim given to him must be so trained that they are permanently anchored on the positive side of life.

The final aim of all this will be to make the child independent. The acid test of any educational system is the extent to which it succeeds in bringing the child to educate himself. A way of attaining this aim which has stood the test of years will be shown in the practical part of this book.

CHAPTER II

Discipline Without Punishment

In this chapter we will consider some of the more elementary devices for controlling a class and go on to outline the way in which we would handle a boy who is a general nuisance.

A school class is primarily a matter of mass instruction. We do not propose to deal in detail here with the problem of turning this mass into a more organic kind of community. This may happen of itself on occasions. A class, for example, may become concentrated and knit together by its interest in the subject of a lesson, and the better the teacher the more frequently will he succeed in bringing this about. When this happens, the class feels and wills as one; it experiences itself as a dramatic ensemble and may justly be said to have developed from a mass into a community. In general, however, when dealing with a class we are dealing with a crowd, and putting all hair splitting aside, we propose to refer to it as a mass.

Where we are faced, not with a class community, but with a mass, there is only one thing for us to do; to establish and maintain discipline as the precondition of every mass institution. Let us consider, by means of examples, some simple devices which enable the teacher to do this.

For the first time the class is taken into the physics laboratory. Instead of the usual forms there are seats. It is not too much to suppose that the children will try out this new-fangled type of seating accommodation from every possible angle.

In such a situation, the teacher can call to his aid the device of anticipation. Before the class sits down he can announce: 'Of course, some of you will imagine that these seats are made for sitting on. How wrong you are! (General astonishment.) They are really a substitute for see saws. Whoever has never see sawed properly isn't a real

31

man. That's the first principle of physics. (Laughter.) But the second principle is even more amusing. Whoever hasn't mastered the principle of balance gets a bad mark in physics. That, of course, means every boy who falls off his seat.' (More laughter.)

The children settle down more easily after some such little speech because they recognize that the teacher sympathizes with their excitement over the new seats and they are therefore more prepared to make a co-operative return.

Again, the children are to visit a museum. It is reasonable to assume that the children will have varying interests and that the visit will be attended by some disorder. The teacher therefore says:

'John sees a ship and would like to sail in it. So he rushes up to it at once. Theodore sees a working model of a pump, and he rushes up to that. Andrew sees a dragonfly and cranes his head until someone bumps into him and he falls over. One or two others fall over him until no one knows whether it is a game of sardines or a school class on a visit to a museum. Yes, visiting a museum is a silly thing to do. Every boy has the chance to behave in any way he likes.'

The teacher can be quite certain that at this point one or two voices will be heard protesting, and he will immediately utilize these interruptions: 'What? Isn't that so? What ought we to do then? Stay together? Why? Oh, in order to learn something. Really? I thought perhaps that it was just for a rough and tumble that we had come here. However, if you think otherwise, we had better get ourselves organized.'

Whoever thinks that none of the children will now let his eyes stray to other things has no idea about how children behave and is beyond all help. The aim of such devices is not to establish iron discipline, but at least they deprive the greater part of the mass of its tendency to become disruptive. The teacher takes up towards the anticipated consequences an ironical attitude which at the same time is not unfriendly. In parenthesis, it may be said that irony can be a dangerous weapon because it is all too easy to hurt children and arouse their resentment. As a habit on the part of the teacher, especially if it develops into sarcasm, it may quickly destroy all hope of good relationships. Only a teacher who is in such close contact with the children that they can always hear the agreeable background music of his sympathy for them against the pointed acidity of the theme can use irony with success.

In the two examples which we have just given, it was a question of an improvisation in the face of anticipated trouble. And here, as in all circumstances, it is some kind of preparatory organization which is the chief means of preserving discipline. Much disorder can be prevented by means of preparatory organization as exercised by the teacher or as delegated to class leaders, group leaders, monitors or others. For example, the list of those present and of those who come late may be kept by one special boy, who also draws up a graph of the attendances. But all this preparatory organization can be effective only on one condition—that of consistency. Whoever carries out the method for a time and then neglects it when it begins to be effective lets slip a means of preventing a hundred and one disagreeable happenings.

But what is to be done if, owing to insufficient foresight or insufficient organization, indiscipline, disorder or revolt have already developed? Here again it is well to make the situation clear on the basis of examples.

The teacher faces his class. The children in general pay attention, but there are one or two who feel they must first look for something or other in their desks, or hurriedly finish off whatever they were saying. In short, instead of order there is vague chaos. The children are by no means alert and ready. Then—even if it isn't altogether true— the teacher observes: 'Group—whatever the number may be—is looking very business-like this morning.' In a few seconds the class is in the best possible order. The teacher has used the device of presenting the class with the opposite picture.

The device of splitting the worst offenders off from the rest operates quite differently. It goes something like this. In the break the class is literally bubbling over and its attitude can hardly be described as anything but undisciplined. Some of the children begin to climb over and race round the desks and the danger of injuries becomes acute.[1] The teacher must now intervene to prevent still worse excesses. He picks out two of the worst offenders: 'Richard! John! Come into the corridor!' That has the effect of a cold shower. Common sense returns and the class sobers down. However, it is clear that with this the situation is not permanently resolved. The teacher has to use the respite quickly to get purposeful activity going.

A situation which is developing in such a fashion may also make it necessary for the teacher to use a different method: a sharp order

---

[1] It will be remembered that these children have no playground (v. Introduction).

immediately suppressing all resistance. For example: 'Sit down, all of you!' We must pause a moment or two here, though, in order to avoid misunderstanding. First of all, anyone who thinks that he can maintain discipline by shouting out orders from time to time is quite wrong, and, incidentally, he is his own worst enemy. If anyone were to ask me for the shortest recipe for maintaining discipline I would answer 'unfailing calmness'. That may seem to be in strange contradiction to the advice just given to issue a sharp and definite order. But if we ask ourselves why an occasional sharp order produces the desired effect at once, the apparent contradiction is solved: the sharp order has an immediate effect precisely because it is in strong contrast to the teacher's usual attitude and the children realize it at once. The secret of its effect likes precisely in this contrast. But once again, the sharp order is not the end of the matter. Once discipline has been restored we do not go on by uttering reproaches or perhaps threats. Instead the teacher will say: 'It's a pity that you forced me to adopt such a disagreeable tone. It isn't often heard in our class. Think over why that is so and we'll deal with the question at our next discussion of class-matters. I shall be anxious to hear your opinion.'

Another very useful device is that of identification. The class is about to go off to the projection room to see a film. The boys are already gathered in the corridor. Then comes the disagreeable news that for some reason or other we can't go and that we shall have to get on with a normal lesson. Naturally there is a great disappointment and even some indignation. The children march back into class unwillingly and full of inner resentment. One or two of them fling themselves down into their desks. Revolt is in the air.

The teacher faces the class and says out loud:

'What a stupid thing! We've got to sit here now.' He walks up and down once or twice and then stops.

'What are we going to do now?'

The identification of the teacher with the children has already resolved the resistance in most of them. 'Very well, what are we going to do now?' One of the boys suggests discontentedly, 'Let's read something then.' The teacher shakes his head. 'Let's eat then.' The teacher again shakes his head. Then he declares mysteriously, 'I've got a much better idea. Let's sit here for an hour and bore ourselves because we've got to sit here. Who would like to make a start?'

That is the device of irony properly used. The incipient revolt is liquidated.

34

Or again, the teacher comes into the class. There is a certain amount of suppressed giggling. The reason for it is not apparent. Then the door of the class cupboard opens and the smallest boy in the class is discovered sitting there. He rolls out amidst a storm of laughter. There is only one thing for the teacher to do, identify himself with the class, laugh with the rest.

Minor matters, certainly. But added up, they amount to the art of maintaining discipline without tears. Where such superficial measures do not first clear the way, it will hardly be possible to carry through the real and profounder work of education subsequently.

And now let us turn to the problem of a particular child who makes persistent difficulties that upset the class. The children assemble at a quarter to eight on the ground floor of the school. As the teacher walks through their ranks he notices a more or less suppressed giggling. He pays no particular attention to it and goes off to his room. No sooner has he closed the door behind him than he hears a loud burst of laughter and much trampling. When he opens the door he is just in time to see several boys rushing up from the cellar. Investigation of the circumstances reveals the following:

One of the boys, Rupert, had stood quietly in his place for a while. The school caretaker then went down into the basement to the boiler-room. At that moment Rupert had a mischievous idea: 'Why not go down into the cellar too?' He made the suggestion to one or two boys who stood near him and down they all went, with Rupert in the lead.

Asked by the teacher what they had intended to do in the cellar the delinquents chorused: 'Nothing!' They were certainly telling the truth and it was perfectly obvious that up to then it had not occurred to them that such an action ought to have some cogent reason. They hadn't thought about it at all; they had just gone with the rest. But the 'ringleader'—and the difference between a ringleader and a real leader is made very clear here—hadn't thought about it either, and he was quite unable to give any sensible reason for his action. It had 'just come into his mind'. That was all. The only real motive behind it all was a desire to do something prohibited. If it had all gone off without discovery then the boys would have laughed about the exploit for a long time to come and the ringleader would have been the hero of the occasion—which was in accordance with his secret lifestyle—earning, at very little expense, the admiration of all for his amusing prank. The incident was, of course, amusing; that was proved by the half-suppressed giggling. Although only a small group of the boys took a direct part in the prank, all of them did in spirit.

We may usefully follow some more situations involving Rupert. Lessons are about to begin. The boys are seated at their desks preparing their things for the first lesson. Set-squares and drawing-boards are new departures in the class and the boys are a little unclear as to their uses. The teacher is in the corridor talking to one of the mothers. From the classroom he hears a crack. Then another one. Before he can walk the few steps to the classroom to see what is happening, the noise develops into a storm, which ceases at once as soon as he appears in the doorway. What has happened?

From the report of the class leader and from the evidence of Rupert himself the following facts emerge. Rupert had held up his set-square and dropped it accidentally. It had fallen on to his drawing-board with an agreeable crack. That was the chance beginning. Rupert immediately picked up his set-square and repeated the performance deliberately, at the same time looking round at the others triumphantly. And then other boys had followed his example. Soon the whole class was either doing it or laughing as the others did it. Once again an amusing prank for which the boys had to thank Rupert.

A school outing is in progress. The class goes down a wooden incline. Almost imperceptibly the pace grows faster. Suddenly Rupert's voice sounds: 'Hurrah! Charge!' And the whole class stampedes down the hill at a gallop. More and more children are caught up in the rush. Loud shouting is heard and now the whole class is thundering up hill and down dale until the presence of a road causes common sense to return. Now all the boys stand there gasping, but delighted. It was lovely to break through the bonds of discipline like that. What a lad Rupert is, to be sure! Always full of bright ideas!

Probably every teacher has had to cope with a boy of this kind whose presence constantly threatens to upset the class in spite of every measure taken to organize its activities and to forestall opportunities for indiscipline. If only for the sake of the class and for his own peace, the teacher is now compelled to consider the problem of this particular boy. He has to win this boy back to co-operation with the rest and he is bound to take on to a certain extent the role of the psychologist. Let us therefore take four specific punishment situations in which this boy was involved, analyse them, and show how the attitude which inspired them may be changed without recourse to punishment, to the benefit not only of the boy himself, but of the class of which he is a member.

1. Rupert has often to be called to account because of his inattention. Again and again his mind wanders off to other things. During an arithmetic lesson he is observed stuffing a long strip of paper into his mouth to the great amusement of all the boys around him. Everyone begins to look at Rupert, who is now pulling the endless strip of paper out of his mouth like a conjurer. There is a burst of laughter. The whole class is upset. A punishment situation has clearly arisen.

2. The work of the children is being checked. The children present fair copies of the composition they have written the day before at school. Rupert has not made a fair copy, although his composition was a good one. Reason advanced: 'I forgot.' Another boy declares that on a visit to his house he reminded Rupert of the work. Thus there is both laziness and lying. A punishment situation has arisen.

3. One of the boys in the class has been given a new fountain-pen with a very fine point. The next day the fountain-pen has disappeared. A few days later Rupert is discovered in possession of the pen. He has tried to disguise it by screwing on a cap of a different colour. Rupert has robbed a comrade and a punishment situation has arisen.

4. In a handicraft lesson another boy accidentally smears paste on a folder Rupert has been making. In the next break Rupert attacks the boy and gives him such a blow that his mouth begins to bleed and his underlip is swollen. A punishment situation has arisen.

Now what really lies behind all this? Rupert is almost twelve. He was brought up on the bottle and he still shows signs of rickets. He was late in walking and late in talking. His father suffers from lung trouble and the family is poor. The mother has to go out to work and she is therefore away from the house during the day. At the age of two, Rupert was sent to his grandmother in the country because the father had to go into hospital and there was no one at home to look after the child. In the hands of his grandmother he was excessively mollycoddled. Until he was six years old she would take him on her lap to feed him. He slept in his grandmother's bed with her arms round him. The mother declares: 'If he wakes up at night and doesn't feel an arm around him he screams pitifully.' Thus Rupert has been very badly prepared for the subsequent task of establishing proper relations with his fellow human beings, relations which require both give and take.

37

At the age of six Rupert leaves this hot-house atmosphere of excessive tenderness at his grandmother's house and returns to his parents. He is kept away from his father on account of the danger of contagion. All day long he is left to his own devices. When his mother returns home from her day's work, he makes life hard for her by creating all sorts of difficulties, particularly by refusing to eat properly. The mother reacts to this by severe punishments. Rupert's tyrannical reign is threatened. The struggle for power begins. At school he becomes noticeable by his lack of ability to concentrate. He is restless, more inclined to play than work, and he compels the teacher to pay constant attention to him. In addition, he is left-handed, has very little manual dexterity, and finds great difficulty in learning to write. When he is moved up to the next class a little sister is born. All the outward symptoms of his struggle for power are then intensified. 'After that his behaviour at home was almost impossible,' his mother tells us.

The general experience that children who have been mollycoddled in their early years are particularly bad at arithmetic is confirmed in the case of Rupert. He disliked arithmetic intensely, and in the elementary school[1] his teachers have frequent cause to complain that he lives in his imagination; that he is no good at all at arithmetic and that he shows almost a fear of the arithmetic lesson. The inevitable and thoroughly discouraging influence of the mother—'You'll never be anything at school because all you think of is playing the fool and annoying other people'—and the repeated experience of failure (conditioned by the organic disposition to left-handedness, his inadequate preparation for school and his inability to train his own forces) all make the child despair of ever finding a positive solution for the problem of 'school'. As Rupert cannot believe in the possibility of respect for him at school he has to be content with 'attention' in its place. His efforts are directed towards making himself the centre of attention as cheaply as possible.

Let us now examine the above described punishment situations a little more closely.

1. We now understand that his antics with the strip of paper are performed in order to win him success on the cheap. The boys who laugh at his antics seem to be on his side. For a moment or two he experiences a feeling of triumph; he has not mastered his task, but he

---

[1] The elementary school (Grundschule) embraces the first to fourth school years (six to ten years) in Austria.

has side-stepped his difficulties. He has astonished others and made them admire him; he is 'king' in a world of fantasy. One of his compositions, which we produce here, clearly reveals his secret aim in life:

'Once I had a special dream. I was lying on a king's throne asleep. Then I heard music which woke me up. I saw many servants coming towards me. I looked more carefully and I saw that one servant was carrying a golden crown. And I thought: "That crown is mine! It belongs to me." The servant came up to me and said: "Greetings, King!" And then he put the crown on my head. Then I got up and went down with them. Suddenly I stumbled and fell down. I woke up and found myself on the floor. What a pity it wasn't real!'

2. Rupert has 'forgotten' to make a fair copy of his otherwise good composition. It will be remembered that he has great difficulties with writing because he is left-handed. He tries to escape from a task which he feels he is unable to perform. Individual Psychology is well acquainted with this form of 'forgetting accidentally on purpose'. It knows all the tricks used to avoid doing something unpleasant whilst inventing excuses for the avoidance, thereby leaving the personality undiminished. 'Oh, no! I'm not too cowardly to tackle difficult tasks; it's just that I forgot. If I didn't suffer from such forgetfulness you'd soon see what I could do. . . .' As long as Rupert needs this forgetfulness in order to bolster up his opinion of himself no amount of reminders on the part of others will succeed in persuading him not to 'forget'.

And Rupert was not really lying when he said he had forgotten. Despite the reminder given him by a classmate he had actually 'forgotten'. The very next minute the reminder had gone out of his head. Individual Psychology knows how the mind operates to exclude anything from consciousness which tends to militate against the life style.

Perhaps someone will object that Rupert didn't really forget and the reason was sheer laziness? But this assumption puts us back precisely where we were before. Is 'laziness' anything else but an attitude which protects self-esteem and evades the necessity of doing something positive? We must therefore look behind the symptoms to the sickness itself, and that sickness is profound discouragement in the face of the tasks demanded by life.

3. Rupert has stolen something from a comrade. When he is caught, he explains: 'I tried the pen and I could write so well with it.' His

explanation is illuminating: 'My classmate writes nicely. But he has a fountain-pen with a fine point. That's what does it, the fine point. If I had a fountain-pen like that I'd show them. . . . It's my bad pen which makes me write badly. You are always saying that I don't want to write properly. You're wrong. You see, I'm even prepared to steal a fountain-pen in order to be able to write properly. But if you take the pen away from me now then I shan't be responsible for my bad handwriting any more. It will be your fault. . . .'

4. Rupert is physically much stronger than the boy he attacked, and his outburst was therefore a clear 'appeal to force'. Because his work was damaged, even accidentally, Rupert felt that he had suffered a defeat, and as that threatened his self-esteem he immediately became aggressive.

Attack and retreat—Rupert uses both tactics to bolster up his self-esteem, which he despairs of maintaining or increasing by any positive and objective performance of the tasks life imposes on him. We now understand Rupert's life style and, because we understand it, his reactions in the four punishment situations we have described are no longer a mystery to us.

Let us assume that we resort to punishment. Perhaps in case No. 1 we could prevent Rupert from continuing to disturb the class. But that would be contenting ourselves with superficial success. Would we really have succeeded in making him more attentive? Let us further assume that by punishment we forced him to pay attention and thus managed to repress the symptom. Would the boy, despite all his enforced attention, really master his arithmetic as long as his discouragement led him to believe that he could not succeed? And even if we put the best possible complexion on the case and assume that in consequence of his enforced attention Rupert really does arrive at an experience of success, and that—without any particular Individual Psychological treatment—this generates courage and enables him to master his difficulty, we still cannot be satisfied even with the complete disappearance of the symptom. We must still ask ourselves: has anything really changed in his fundamentally egoistic, anti-social attitude? Perhaps Rupert really will become an acceptable mathematician in later life, but we should not forget that such ability, even if achieved, can still be misused to the disadvantage of others.

There is no doubt that by punishment a child can be forced to pay attention. But there is equally no doubt that at the same time such a child is being accustomed to regard all human relations from the 'superior-inferior' angle and is thus being trained in a basic neurotic attitude. We cannot therefore be satisfied with the disappearance of mere symptoms. On the contrary, our aim is to influence the child's life style for good, to dismantle his egoism and to renew his courage, perhaps by means of organizing some event which brings him an experience of success. If we can, we shall try to make the community in which the child lives a helper in these efforts, and we shall act in a given situation only in relation to the individual and the community.

The individual treatment of Rupert may best be guided by these considerations. Above all, we must first establish contact with him. That is easily done because, thanks to the teacher's calm, objective and invariably friendly attitude, there is already an atmosphere in the class which is favourable to contact. The teacher deliberately ignores some of Rupert's failings and from time to time he will express appreciation of minor positive performances on Rupert's part, and so on.

Then Rupert's secret aim in life must be laid bare. This is done in a personal chat with him.

We talk to the child about the time when he lived with his grandmother and how he got on then. We show him how his grandmother fulfilled all his wishes and how he gradually came to believe that all adults existed merely in order to serve him. We make him conscious of the fact that he has fashioned his relations to his fellow human beings on the understanding that he is to play the role of ruler, of 'king'.

The teacher might say: 'And so you did your best to see to it that your grandmother always had to do what you wanted, and you already knew how to do it. Sometimes you flattered her, sometimes you wept, and sometimes you made disagreeable scenes. And your grandmother always gave in. She was defeated and you were the victor. Before you had to go to school you thought that your grandmother and all the other grown-ups existed only for you, and that they all had to do whatever you wanted. I am not surprised that you thought like that. Perhaps I should have thought in just the same way as you if I had been in your place. (Relief.) But it was a mistake for all that! And you are still entangled in that mistake today.'

We go on to show Rupert that 'being king' is still his secret wish even today and we interpret his dream for him. We show him how he is mourning for his lost kingship—'What a pity it wasn't real!' And we show him how in the present situation of harsh reality with a stern mother and a school which expects attainment from him he is trying to keep up at least the appearance of being 'superior'.

'You aren't very good at your sums even now, are you?' the teacher might go on, 'And because you feel that you can't be a victor in sums, that you can't be really "superior", you go in for such antics as the performance with the strip of paper. When all the others laugh at it and seem to admire you for being such a daring fellow, you feel that you are a hero, after all. But it's only an outward appearance. In reality you are running away like a coward; running away from your sums. And I know why. You run away because you think sums are much too difficult for you ever to do. But that's just where you are very much mistaken. Anyone can learn to do sums.' (Encouragement.)

We reveal the real reason of his inattention and we discuss his difficulties in writing. Here too we show him how he is trying to run away from his difficulties. When we discuss his theft he sees his own motives for the first time. We know, of course, that only one who can see through all his own tricks and arrangements to evade the tasks of life can ever educate himself, and that only this self-realization can become the basis of self-education, which, in the last resort, must be the aim of all education.

Experiences of success must be organized for Rupert. In the general greyness of his school work there is one bright spot: he reads well. Here is an opportunity to insert the lever. He is appointed helper to another boy who cannot read very well. Now this boy, though a poor reader, is a good writer, and he is appointed helper to Rupert in writing. For the first time, Rupert really takes himself in hand.

The following comments written in Rupert's exercise book are intended to show the attempts to make the boy more and more conscious of his behaviour:

(a) 'Why are you always trying to prove that you just aren't capable of taking yourself in hand for a whole hour on end? The first page is excellently written. This page says: "Look how well I can write when I want to!" But after that you begin to scribble. And the other pages say: "You see, I could when I wanted to, but I am suffering from a sickness called impatience and there is nothing to be done about it." However, I just don't believe that. What the scribbled pages say isn't true. There is no sickness called impatience. That's

42

just an excuse. The truth is that you are still trying to run away from something difficult. And do you know why you are doing that? Because you haven't enough confidence in yourself. It seems that I have a higher opinion of you than you have of yourself. No matter how often you may try to prove that you just have no persistence—I don't believe it. I believe in your ability.'

(b) 'The things that can be done even in a single lesson! I am sure you are astonished yourself at how well you can work when you try. Can you feel how you are growing? I think the reason for it is that Richard is helping you and you are helping Richard. He is beginning to read much better and you are beginning to write much better. That's what I call a real friendship! Real friends don't encourage each other to play the fool all the time; they really help each other. And each friend is glad when the other makes progress.'

[margin note: peer support + mutual help.]

Rupert's handwriting improved very considerably, and to improve his arithmetic as well he himself asked for extra lessons. Before long he was beginning to make progress in arithmetic too. Whilst exercising influence on his parents, we renewed his courage and opened the way for comradely relations between him and his classmates. Gradually the demands made on him were increased. After a year his inattentiveness had almost disappeared, and so had most of the other difficulties.

In this transformation, group influence played a part. Rupert's class had a discussion once a week. The affair with the strip of paper naturally came up for discussion and the boys came to the conclusion, on their own initiative, that boys who played the fool were usually boys who did badly at their lessons. They also decided that 'in reality' no one was doing such boys a good service by laughing at their tricks approvingly.

The fact that Rupert had not brought in his homework gave the class an opportunity to discuss 'forgetfulness' and the various motives which made children neglect their work.

The discussion of the fountain-pen episode was particularly illuminating. Quite a number of children recognized that they had the same motives as Rupert. One in particular declared that now he could understand how it came about that he, who was bad at drawing, was always wanting new pencils and crayons. And the boy whose fountain-pen Rupert had stolen proposed that the teacher should have a word with Rupert's father to see if he couldn't buy Rupert a fountain-pen as well.

When the attack on the smaller boy came up for discussion the class dealt with a number of similar situations and in each case the right and the wrong solutions were worked out.

In the almost classic formula of one of the boys: 'Our teacher never punishes and yet he's much stricter. He demands much more.' These words might almost serve to characterize the educational procedure of Individual Psychology.

CHAPTER III

Learning by the Discussion Method

The encouragement of pupils to learn by finding out the facts for themselves may be described as the 'active method' of education. It can be contrasted with the 'passive method' of inculcating instruction into pupils who are required merely to absorb what their teachers or their textbooks put before them. The active method is by no means an innovation in the field of education, and as we have not set out to write a pedagogical textbook, there is no need to list the numerous ways in which it has been put into practice nor the varying results which have been obtained. We need only outline what, in our experience, seem to be the advantages and the limitations of the method.

In principle the active method cannot but win our assent. 'The basis of all education,' it has been said,[1] 'is the individuality of the pupil, and its ultimate object is the "worthwhile personality" and the "worthwhile society". The individual must himself do the decisive work for his own education; all other people can do is to help him. Education is fundamentally self-education.'[1]

The great advantage of the active method lies, then, in the training which it may offer the pupil to think for himself and to develop into an independent human being. But it would be a fallacy to imagine that the method constitutes the whole answer to the problem of self-development. We can show best by means of an example the kind of situation in which its limitations in this respect are to be felt.

Alfred, coming from the lower school into the higher, is a good average pupil, but in one subject he fails completely: mathematics. All the efforts of the teacher meet with no success. Alfred sits and

[1] Paul Fickert: *Didaktik der neuen Schule, Zieckfeld,* Verlag Osterwieck. S,1/2.

looks despairingly at his sums. The more the teacher occupies himself with Alfred the less Alfred seems to understand. The teacher has the feeling of being up against a brick wall. In geography Alfred does quite well until he meets with some numerical relation, for instance a reckoning of measurement, and then he is utterly floored. The same thing happens in physics and chemistry. It is almost as though Alfred had adopted the avoidance of all figures as a rule of life.

The Individual Psychologist, Ida Löwy, of Vienna, has coined the phrase 'stupidity as a means of escape'. And so let us ask ourselves the question in another way: Why is Alfred 'stupid' in sums? And let this question guide our investigations. We then discover that Alfred's father is managing clerk in a big Viennese business house, and as such he is particularly skilled at figures. The mother, a very intelligent woman, tells us that even before Alfred went to school his father was in the habit of saying: 'When you go to school you must do your lessons well, and particularly your sums, because you know Daddy has to do a lot of sums, and when you're big he'll take you to the office with him and then you'll sit at the big writing-desk where Daddy sits now. But you will have to be able to do your sums nicely. That's the great thing.'

For six years Alfred was the only child, and he was rather spoiled by both his parents. Then another baby arrived, a girl, and Alfred was suddenly dethroned. His jealousy showed itself in various ways, and occasionally, without provocation, he would slap his sister's face. She developed into a curly-headed and delightful child. What the mother said was illuminating: 'My husband dotes on the child to this day. He does everything she wants. When she was smaller he would play "Lions and Tigers" with her when he came home from the office. The rumpus the two made! But he paid less and less attention to the boy. In the lower class it wasn't so bad, but when he was in the higher class he pulled his sister away from his father one day and said: "You go away from Daddy now. He's got to help me, otherwise I shan't be able to do my sums." My husband did help him. The next day he came again: "My sums are so difficult. Help me, Daddy." And ever since my husband sits and helps him with his sums, but still the boy makes no progress.' And in answer to the teacher's question: 'And what does his little sister do now?' she replied: 'Oh, she has to get along on her own.'

The situation is already quite clear. Alfred is using his 'stupidity' at sums to win back his father, who had drifted away from him on the arrival of his sister. Whilst the father is busy helping him with his sums he cannot pay attention to the sister. What methods of instruction can possibly teach Alfred to do his sums so long as he uses his inability in an attempt to win back the affection and attention of the father he fears he has lost? It is now quite clear to us that all efforts must be in vain even if now and again Alfred does succeed in doing a sum correctly. And it is also clear why in such a case the 'active method' can produce no positive results.

The case shows why Individual Psychology considers it necessary to utter a warning. The active method in itself does not educate the individual to positive, spiritual attitudes, that is to say to attitudes which encourage the development of the personality and co-operation with the community. The active method constantly affords opportunities for adopting such attitudes, *but that is all it does.* Whether a child adopts them or not depends on his experience of the work and on his own attitude to it. And this attitude towards work depends entirely upon the child's style of life, that is to say, upon the degree of his community feeling, of his urge to assert himself, of his courage.

Having entered this proviso, we can go on to consider some of the practical problems raised by the active method. In our opinion, this method is best conducted in the form of a free discussion in which all the members of the class can take part. In free discussion, the child's faculties are in the service not only of the objective problems set by the lesson; in the course of solving these he has also to solve the subjective problem of his adaptation to his fellow pupils and to the community at large. This double enlistment of his faculties has always seemed to Individual Psychology to be peculiarly valuable. The child is being trained at one and the same time for his work in the world and for his place in the community. And his interest in the work before him is being stimulated not only by the work itself but also by the working community of which he is a member.

But we have to recognize that the discipline difficulties which arise when the method of free discussion among the children is used can be such as to reduce its educational success to a minimum. Whoever has had practical experience of this method will admit that the difficulties are very great, and if we still ask teachers to persevere with the method we are obliged to offer them ways and means of overcoming them. This we shall do in a subsequent chapter. For the moment, we will concentrate upon describing the method itself.

Learning by the Discussion Method

Let us suppose that we are about to take a class. The children are already sitting in groups. The reading lesson begins. When the reading is over, silence automatically descends. Now the class work starts. One boy perhaps will get up. He does not address himself to the teacher, but to another pupil: 'What does this mean. . . ?' or 'It says here. . . .' or, 'I don't understand. . . .' Once such a question has been put, once a boy has expressed some idea in connection with a word, an expression, or the theme itself, or has brought forward an illustrative example from his own experience, the discussion begins. For example, a boy who has two brothers, one of them a stepbrother, seeks to make the relationship of stepchildren clear to the others. Other children take part in the discussion. Although the question has already been clearly answered the discussion still goes on and there is a danger that the class will lose itself in a jungle of family relationships. That must be prevented. The part of the teacher is generally confined to guiding the discussion and indicating such points as are worthy of more detailed treatment. This he does simply by putting in a word here and there, or by asking a question.

Very often the class work will be interrupted or replaced by group work along the same lines. For instance, we come across the expression 'in dire need': the class is then divided into a number of groups, and five minutes are allotted for the groups to think up similar expressions. By setting a time limit in this way the class is encouraged to apply itself, although of course, such a time limit is not always set. At the end of the five minutes the leader of each group reads out the results:

Group One: Dire need. Hard times. Bitter fate. Cruel anger. Bad conscience. And so on.

Group Two: Dire need. Lack of bread. Hard toil. Bad temper. Fierce anger. And so on.

Group Three: Dire need. Bad end. Hard work. Fierce anger. Bitter life. And so on.

Group Four: Dire need. Bitter hunger. Hard struggle. Firm purpose. Blind anger. And so on.

The general discussion opens up again and we are once more working as a class. Each pupil now takes the results of the joint work and uses them for himself, notes down the new expressions and thus widens his vocabulary.

Another example: the lesson begins; silently the teacher writes on the blackboard: 'What we observe with our senses.' The debate begins at once. The children note down physiological-psychological problems in their exercise books, such as: 'How do we see?' The title of these books is *Unsolved Problems*. From time to time we take a look at them, and often we find a question that we can solve at once. Such a book is known in the language of the class as 'The Ice-Box'. Through the discussion we soon come to adjectives. And now to group work again: 'What do we observe without eyes, ears, etc?' The group work is then summed up in the class as a whole. The discussion goes further: how can nouns be turned into adjectives? A proposal arises: 'Let us see what suffixes we need to do it with.' Group work again: three 'factories' for the production of adjectives are set up. Three minutes' production time! Result:

Group One: Thirsty, hungry, greedy, dirty, and so on.

Group Two: Childish, womanly, foolish, and so on.

Group Three: Happy, childish, womanly, wonderful, daily, and so on.

Then control and note-taking.

Pupil: 'And then we can put an adjective to every noun!'

Teacher: 'What do you mean exactly?'

Pupil: 'Well, a fortunate man, for instance.'

Several Pupils: 'Let's do it!'

Teacher: 'Right you are, if you want to.'

Result: the adjective used as a supplement to the noun.

The composition lesson is characterized by individual work (draft, writing out and subsequent reading) and class work (discussion and criticism). Dramatization is also a suitable subject for joint work, and the following is an example.

After a lesson in the history of Greece the class has read a number of Greek sagas, including the story of Hercules at the cross roads. In the subsequent discussion the children gave many examples of how they had often stood at the cross roads, and how they had come to the conclusion that there was always a 'hard' and an 'easy' way. Finally, one boy expressed the opinion that it was much more difficult to do one's exercises than to play football. The teacher now intervened with the suggestion that the tempting of a child to evade its work could be presented in a dramatic form. A number of children now began to extemporize. The drastic methods they proposed to tempt a fellow-pupil away from his work to play football caused a good deal of laughter in the class and finally a proposal was made that such a game should be written down. The work began and had already progressed beyond the introduction when one youngster objected: 'But that isn't a proper theatrical piece. It ought to have at least three acts.' General consternation! In the silence another youngster burst out: 'All right then, let's do it in three acts.' After some further discussion, which became quite excited at times, a plan was adopted: 'Thanks to his acquaintance with the saga of Hercules a boy is to be persuaded to choose the 'hard' way.' New objection on the part of one of the boys: 'You can't go at it like a bull at a gate and just let the teacher read out the saga.' Another boy: 'I once saw a film, and there what a man had to say was really played on the screen.' General agreement: 'That's how we'll do it!' Decision (according to the apt definition of one of the boys): 'Hercules at the cross roads will be played—and the rest of it too.'

At this point the teacher ventures an objection: 'If someone is to be changed, then before the change he must have been different. How is the audience to realize that a person has been changed?' New realization: 'In the first act we must show how the boy in question first thought.' With this the plan of the piece was finished, the problem phase had been overcome. We were now able to begin with the detailed work of the solution phase. The children produced ideas, suggestions and proposals. Much of it was simply ignored as unusable. Useful contributions were noted down. Inadequate proposals were licked into shape, added to, given an improved style and then written down. The teacher lost no opportunity to point out that credit was not due only to the boy who found the final formulation of an idea, but also to those who had proposed it in the first place or contributed to it. With this he encouraged the will of the children to contribute 'bricks', and the work went on through about eight lessons. The following is the final result. All that has been changed is one or two dialect expressions that would not be generally understandable.

'HERCULES AT THE CROSS-ROADS'

I

(Meadow in the foreground. Wood in the background. A school class approaches. It arrives singing. John and Frank sit down in the foreground.)

John: 'Phew! It's hot today!'

Frank: 'Well, let's go and lie down in the shade.'

John: 'I'd like to do nothing but lie down all day.'

Frank: 'What have you got there?'

John: 'Something fine! A liver-paste sandwich.'

Frank: 'Let me taste. Oh, that's good. Give me a bit!'

John: 'There's another bit for you, just to show you I'm not greedy. My mother works hard, but she's got time to look after me.'

Frank: 'I haven't got a mother any more. .... She died two years ago.'

John: 'I'm sorry for you. What are you going to be when you grow up?'

Frank: 'Well, I don't know. I'll have to be a labourer, I suppose.'

John: 'When I grow up I'm going to take it easy. I'm not going to work my inside out. But you'll have to work awfully hard to earn a little money.'

Frank: 'You don't want to count your chickens before they're hatched. Perhaps I'll get on better than you think.'

John: 'So you can see the future, can you? Don't you know that everyone's life is already laid down for him?'

Frank: 'No! I don't believe that. Everyone makes his own happiness.'

Teacher (coming forward): 'I overheard what you said. Frank can't explain to you very well just what it is he means, John, because he's still inexperienced. But if you like I'll tell you a story that bears on your two contradictory proverbs.'

John and Frank together: 'Oh, fine!'

The teacher sits down with the two boys.

II

(Mountains in the background. Meadow in the foreground. Where the ways part lies a stone. Hercules comes on to the scene. Stands still, obviously thinking, and then sits down on the stone.)

Hercules: 'Which way shall I go now? Right or left? A difficult decision. If only I knew where these roads led to! If only someone came along who could tell me which is the right one! By Zeus, I've never before been in a position like this! Standing here like a child and not knowing what to do! Nothing but mountains to be seen. This road looks very steep. What's that white thing there? Is it a man? It's probably a cloud. I must have a look at the other road.'

(He pushes aside a bough and goes with long strides to the other road.)

'This way looks easier. There's another white patch. But a much big-

ger one. That can't be a cloud. Is Zeus sending me a messenger perhaps?'
(A white form approaches.)
Hercules: 'Isn't that a woman? Who could it be?'
Voice: 'Hercules! Hercules!'
Hercules: 'What do you want of me?'
Virtue: 'I want to give you advice.'
Voice: 'Hercules! Hercules!'
Hercules: 'Another woman!'
Vice: 'I have come to show you the way.'
Hercules: 'Well, where do these two roads lead?'
Virtue: 'Hercules, take my path. It certainly is not an easy one. It leads up on to a high mountain. On top there is a beautiful view. But the way is steep and stony. You will have to climb hard.'
Vice: 'Hercules, take my path. You won't need to exert yourself. The way goes through a shady wood. It goes down all the time. It leads over flowery fields into a shady valley.'
Hercules: 'What! As a hero I should take the easy way?'
Virtue: 'Hercules, you are right. Take the path that leads to happiness.'
Vice: 'Don't be deceived, Hercules. My path will lead you to real happiness.'
Hercules (springing to his feet): 'Which road shall I take?' (He looks first at one and then at the other.) 'Actually your way looks the more beautiful, Vice.'
(Vice grins.)
Vice to Virtue: 'You see. He will go my way. And it's much more convenient.'
Virtue: 'Hercules, you, of all people, propose to go over soft meadows and flowery meads like an old woman! And you call yourself a hero? You should be ashamed of yourself! You, who, as a child, strangled snakes! And now you're so cowardly! Shame on you, Hercules! If you take my path you will have many adventures. You will strangle lions. You will drag the hound of hell from the underworld and you will fight against dragons. And when you have overcome all obstacles the gods will accept you.'
Vice: 'Why go to all that trouble? Why risk your life? Just in order to be a hero! Don't listen to the babbling voice of Virtue.'
(Hercules is sunk in deep thought and the figures disappear.)
Virtue (from a distance): 'Hercules, Hercules, you, as an ancient hero, stand alone and abandoned in the wide world.

The Heavens await your word:
Take my path and you'll be heard.

Hercules springs to his feet: 'Virtue, I'll take your path.'

III

(John is sitting at a table engaged on his work.)
John: '3 times 8 is 24. 6 times 8 is 48. . . .'
(There is a knock on the door.)
John: 'Come in!'
(Frank and Max come in.)
John: 'Hallo there!'
Frank: 'Hallo yourself.'
Max: 'What are you up to?'
John: 'I'm doing my homework and you'll have to leave me in peace.'
Frank: 'You're right. Get on with it. Take your time and write carefully. In half an hour I'll come back and fetch you. So long!'
Max: 'What a goody-goody! Pitch the stuff aside, John. Come out. Look it's lovely weather outside. The sun is shining. Joseph and Charles are already waiting.'
John: 'No, leave me in peace.'
Max: 'Come on! Charles has got a new football.'
John: 'Go away and let me get on with my work.'
Max: 'But, John, we went to start playing. You're our best player. Don't let us down.'
John puts down his pen and thinks. There is a knock on the door and Frank comes in again.
Frank: 'Aren't you finished yet?'
John: 'Max here wants me to play football instead.'
Frank: 'Think of the story the teacher told us. You want to go the easy way and yet you think you can be something!'
John: 'I suppose you're right.'
Max: 'Fiddlesticks. Don't let yourself be soft-soaped by that goody-goody. What do you get out of it if you do do your homework well? It doesn't matter whether you get a good mark or a bad one, does it? You haven't got a mother to scold you in any case.'
John: 'Do you think I learn for my parents then?'
Max: 'Well, for what else?'
John: 'For my future, of course.'

Max: 'I've never thought of my future.'

Frank: 'Then it's about time you did! I have a friend in the Blind School,[1] and although he's only in the lower class he's already thinking of his profession.'

Max: 'But I'm not blind.'

Frank: 'See! That's just what you are, blind! Your mind is blind. Look: a blind man goes up a mountain, comes to a precipice and tumbles over because he hasn't seen the threatening danger. You don't see the danger threatening you either. You'll end up in misery if you go on as you're going and don't learn anything. Don't you understand that, Max? Are you going to stay blind?'

Max: 'No. Perhaps you're right. But tell me, Frank, isn't it a hard job to learn so much?'

Frank: 'Yes, it is hard, but it's work for the future.'

John (putting down his pen): 'That's finished now and I can go with you, Frank.'

Max: 'Here's the ball, John. I'll take the more difficult path too. I'm going home now—to do my homework.'

John: 'That's the ticket!'

Frank: 'Rather!'

(They all shake hands and the curtain falls.)

The reader will have noticed that the third part of the piece did not turn out as proposed in the original plan. Not John, but Max is converted. The reason for this change was that one of the boys said that both John and Frank had understood the story told by the teacher in any case, and that they should now pass on their knowledge as 'helpers'.

We are a long way from assuming that after the composition of this little play all the children of the class chose 'the hard way', but at the same time we feel that it is not too much to say that the educational effect of this joint work was certainly greater than the teacher could have obtained if he had merely followed the reading of the story with a moral lecture. In this instance we are dealing only with the offer of an opportunity to the children to educate themselves. Some of the children probably took it, the rest probably did not. The educational effect of such things cannot be directly measured.

And now let us go on from the individual case to a general formulation: 'What we must do is to raise the work—all work, because

[1] At that time the class was in close relations with a class in the Blind School.

none is too low or too unimportant—into the moral sphere.'[1] Individual Psychology advocates this ethical note in teaching; not in the sense that it encroaches on the elevated domain of religion, and not in the sense of encouraging moral lectures, which children find merely tiresome, but in the sense of recommending that every possible opportunity should be seized upon in order to build bridges from the subject to the community and to show the motives behind the choosing of the useful or the useless side of life.

We cannot deal with the innumerable possibilities of doing this which offer themselves, but a few examples will make the position clearer. In the teaching of history we encourage the children to think about the fact that civilization and culture were created only by the work of men banded together in a definite aim; we lead them to a clear recognition of the dependence of each individual on the community, and we show the children that the moral level of the individual can be judged and confirmed only by his achievements on behalf of the community. In the geography lesson we bring the children to recognize that the forces of nature can be harnessed only by the will and determination of individuals and the community, and we show them that the heroic deeds of great explorers were conditioned by their will to do the useful thing. In natural science we show the children how scientists studying bacteria often sacrificed themselves in order to serve the community. In the reading lesson when studying the biographies of great men we bring the children to recognize that human courage and tireless work is more important than any decree of fate. With this the instructional work principle is developed further into the sphere of education.

The class as a working community is a training ground for the individual child enabling him on the one hand to perform the tasks demanded of him, and, on the other, to solve the problems of his relations with his fellows. Individual Psychology favours communal work in the school because it gives the child more opportunity of taking part and at the same time makes him realize his dependence on his fellows. The child is thus constantly compelled to take up his own attitude on the basis of this twofold relation to work and to the community. The working community trains the child to work and through work, though within the limits Individual Psychology has already shown.

[1] E. Burger, *Arbeitspädagogik*, p. 325.

CHAPTER IV

Organizing the Lessons

One thing can rightly be demanded in all circumstances and that is that no part, whether large or small, of the time set aside for teaching should be lost in collecting the various requisites for a lesson and making them available. When a lesson begins everything which is required for it should be ready to hand. There is no point in overwhelming the children with rules and regulations, or in trying to settle all the problems of this technical preparation at the first attempt. Efficient technical organization in the school must develop organically.

Let us take an example. The newcomers at our school have already had their first two geography lessons and the third is about to begin. The children are all busily opening their atlases, searching through their satchels to find their geography books, and fiddling about with their pencil boxes. The teacher stands patiently waiting and looks at the clock. At last everyone is ready and the last crayon or pencil which has been dropped is now back in its proper place. The lesson can begin. The teacher looks at the clock and then announces: 'It took you four minutes and twenty-eight seconds to get ready.' After that, no more than a few words are necessary to make the children realize that during the course of a year a simply tremendous amount of time is lost if four and a half minutes are wasted out of every lesson.

Teacher: 'Perhaps one of you who has thoroughly understood what we have been talking about can make a suggestion for improvement.'

No. 12: 'We ought to get our things ready before the lesson begins.'

Teacher: 'And how should that be done exactly?'

No. 26: 'The atlases and the geography books should be ready.'

Teacher: 'In your satchels?'

No. 26: 'No. On the desk in front of us.'

Teacher: 'And what else?'

Several children in chorus: 'Paper for making notes ready. Pencils ready.'

Teacher: 'That's fine! But do you think you can all do that together?'

Many children: 'Oh yes.'

Teacher: 'Yes, I rather think you can. After all, you're all ten years old. Next time I'll come in before the lesson begins and see who's properly ready.'

At the beginning of the next lesson all the children are sitting there looking at the teacher.

Teacher: 'Now I'm really wondering whether you're all ready.' (Goes round and inspects.) 'Yes, really and truly: everyone's ready. Only one of you has his atlas open at the wrong page, but that's probably a mistake.'

This example is sufficient to indicate that the process of obtaining efficient technical preparation goes through several phases. The first step is to make the children realize that time is being unnecessarily wasted. It isn't in the least necessary that all the children should clearly realize this. It is enough if only a few of the children—perhaps even only one—points out: 'In the time we've wasted we could have been learning something.' There is always at least one child like that in a class. Then the teacher says: '*We* have found out something important there.' This observation will then affect many children in a positive sense: they will inwardly approve of the insight won in this way although they did not win it themselves. As many of the children who have been won for the idea now act accordingly, we have obtained our first positive result. A check confirms this.

The check will still confirm a positive success even if a number of the children have failed. The teacher will then make no direct reference to such children, but say: 'Of thirty-two children, twenty-six had everything ready as *we* agreed. These twenty-six children have thus shown that they understood our discussion. I'll note down the number twenty-six, and at our next lesson we'll see whether the number has grown larger or smaller.' Whether the check is carried out by the teacher himself, by one of the children he appoints, or by someone appointed by the children, is not of great importance. The thing that matters is that the check should really be carried out, that each time the actual state of affairs should be publicly recognized,

Organizing the Lessons

and that the great majority of the children should become used to this technical organization of their work.

A second example. In the geography room each of the three windows is provided with a blind. If the lesson demands the showing of a slide then the blinds have to be drawn. Imagine what would happen if the teacher said merely: 'Draw the blinds!' Here, too, the technique must be previously organized.

Teacher: 'I know that you're good and willing boys, but it wouldn't do if I merely said, "Draw the blinds," would it?'

No. 5: 'All of us would dash up to the windows.'

Teacher: 'What can we do to stop that?'

No. 1: 'Three of us should be appointed to do it.'

Teacher: 'Which three?'

No. 7: 'Those who sit near the windows.'

Teacher: 'There's still a weakness there.'

No. 13: 'One of the boys might be absent.'

Teacher: 'Well, what then?'

No. 3: 'We'll appoint a substitute.'

Teacher: 'He might be absent, too.'

(Long silence.)

No. 21: 'Whoever happens to be sitting there should do it.'

Teacher: 'In other words, the job should be attached to the place. And what about the boy to switch off the light?'

Several boys: 'The same with him.'

Teacher: 'There's still a danger though.'

(Again a long silence.)

No. 16: 'We'd squabble over the places because we all want to switch out the light.'

Teacher: 'Well, what shall we do about that?'

No. 28: 'Attach the job to the place. If the boy who sits there is missing not all of us but only one, the next one, takes his place.'

Teacher: 'A very good suggestion. But who is to take the empty place? The boy on the left, the boy behind or the boy in front?'

No. 12: 'The three won't fight about it. What is there in just switching the light out?'

Teacher: 'I'm glad you have such a high opinion of the boys. So have I.'

The rationalization of technique organized in the geography lesson can naturally apply to other subjects, for instance, natural history, history, and so on. It should not be thought that the few minutes taken up with a discussion of ways and means are wasted. On the contrary, the time spent in this way bears rich fruit; a tremendous amount of annoyance, indiscipline, wandering attention and useless officiousness in performing such tasks is avoided. It is an iron law: what the self-governing community fails to rationalize technically will necessarily prove a hindrance to the working community.

Every lesson requires technical preparation. The change from one lesson to the other does not come as easily and naturally as adults are inclined to think. The psychological process of habit plays an important part. But habit presupposes the existence of a certain aim. This will be given by the constantly repeated confirmation of whatever has already been positively achieved. The rationalization of technique is of particular importance in natural science subjects. For instance, experiments by the boys themselves in physics and chemistry are almost impossible without a prearranged order of seating, and unless they already possess a certain degree of manual dexterity. The same is true of drawing and handicraft lessons. In the workshops in particular no useful work can be done unless its preparation is first rationalized.

The class discussions, free as they are, also require to be organized, and certain preliminary rules must be laid down. To put it bluntly: a class discussion will develop none of its potential value if two or more boys are always talking at once, if those who are not speaking are inattentive, if more active and lively pupils give the others no chance of getting a word in edgeways, and if objective criticism is confused with vehemence and rudeness so that in the end the teacher has to shout at the top of his voice to make himself heard above the chaos.

A rational organization of free discussion presupposes:

(1). That not more than one pupil should speak at a time;

(2). That the whole class should pay full attention to whoever is speaking;

(3). That each pupil should have a chance of taking part in the discussion; and

(4). That the teacher should always be in a position to intervene in the discussion and, if necessary, to draw the whole attention of the class to himself.

As all these points are very important we propose to discuss them in detail.

To teach the children to control themselves and to let others speak

59

even when they are burning to get their own say in, to follow up the contribution of a fellow-pupil, or to complement it, to be willing to let themselves be convinced, in short, to be prepared to subordinate themselves to the community, represents an educational problem which is not to be solved from one day to the next or by means of a few technical tricks. The whole complex of educational experience set out in this book is necessary for success. However, to investigate the purely technical side of the problem is an easier matter, and that, and that only, is what we propose to do here.

When suitable seating arrangements allow the children to sit op-

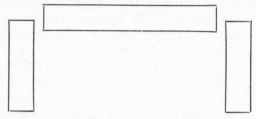

posite each other then they themselves can be brought to formulate the rule in the first lesson or two: 'Anyone wishing to speak must stand up.' The opportunity for securing the adoption of this rule will soon arise, because at first several children will certainly try to talk at once—and succeed, with the result that none of them will be properly understood. However, the mere formulation of this rule will not obviate the evil entirely. Again and again the zeal of individual pupils will run away with them and they will fall back into the old error. If the teacher then delivered a moral lecture on the necessity for self-control, or staged a new demonstration of the disadvantages of more than one person's talking at a time the only result would be a still further waste of time and energy. Naturally, this does not mean that the class should never discuss such things, but if any attempt is made to secure an improvement by threats or punishment then the children will be intimidated and they will hesitate to talk at all. Explosive zeal can certainly be curbed by punishment, but the silence which results will be the silence of the grave. Fortunately, there are other methods and ones which spare the teacher's vocal chords.

The teacher may, in the first place, point out how many children already master the difficult habit of self-control—it is enough to mention a general figure. No names should be mentioned, because that would draw an invidious distinction. Merely to mention a number will allow some of the children to count themselves on the side of virtue. Our own mistakes never bulk very large in our eyes, and this way many a child will obtain an unexpected and very agreeable success experience even though his attitude has been—objectively judged—far from perfect.

Another method is for the teacher to say at the end of the lesson: 'I must make a note of the names of those of you who already know how to take part in a discussion.' But he will mention no names. If the children then want to know the names he will evade a direct answer by saying: 'Each one of you can answer the question for himself by thinking over how he took part in the discussion.' In this way the tension is deliberately maintained.

[margin note: note down names – OK each think individually whether good.]

Again, the teacher may, from time to time, ask the class as a whole: 'Is there anyone in the class you think is making fewer mistakes in the discussion than before?' In this case names are mentioned and a sort of progress record is set up.

[margin note: who has improved & progress record.]

Or a notice drawn by one of the children can be exhibited bearing the words:

[margin note: Notice – reminder]

> **'One at a Time!'**

If two or more children talk at once after that all the teacher has to do is to point to the warning placard. After all, we teachers have very good reason to spare our lungs.

Or irony can be used. The teacher may observe: 'Well, two of you are talking at once. Perhaps another couple would like to join in. And perhaps someone would like to sing.' Or: 'When only three of you talk at once it doesn't make quite enough noise. Let's have a comb-and-paper band, shall we?'

There is also the method of friendly correction: 'Don't you think it would be a good idea if you let someone else talk now and again?'

Or there is the more serious rebuke: 'Sit down and listen for a while instead of pushing yourself forward all the time. There are thirty-five boys in this class, and they all have a right to take part— in fact, it's their duty to take part.' The teacher thus identifies himself with the community and acts only as its mouthpiece.

Another necessary rule, that the whole class should pay attention to whoever is talking, is facilitated to some extent by the seating arrangements indicated. In addition, of course, children will need to be influenced by the teacher in order to encourage them always to give their full attention to whoever is speaking, but the more difficult problem of dealing with really inattentive children does not belong here, because we are dealing only with the technical aspect of these class discussions.

We must see to it that each child is encouraged to take part in the discussion. We must therefore devise some technical means of making it impossible for the children to excuse their lack of co-operation by saying, either to the teacher or their parents: 'I never get a chance of speaking.' This sort of excuse is often used by children to hide their unwillingness to take part and at the same time salve their consciences: 'I wanted to speak, but. . . .' To deal with this sort of thing the teacher can introduce the S.O.S. system. As there was no need for any boy to raise his hand first before taking part in the discussion, we decided to introduce such a signal to help those who found they could not get the floor. After that if one of these less lively children wished to take part he just raised his hand. All the others would then shout: 'S.O.S.!' upon which silence fell and the hand-raiser could talk. This system worked very well. It was introduced in one class and then taken over by others. Of course, the obstinately silent ones cannot be brought to speak even by such technical devices but, at least, once it is made easy for them some children will speak who otherwise would not.

The so-called 'taboo sign' is another technical device, and one the children even find amusing. It consists of some optical or acoustic signal. The teacher raises his hand, or he claps his hands or raps on his desk. The optical signal can be used when the children can see him easily, the acoustic signal when their heads are lowered over their work and the teacher requires their attention immediately. We often use the taboo sign, even when there is no pressing need for it. A little humour can be brought into the thing. The teacher can say: 'That was rather good. Only one boy still flickered his eyelids. The sign didn't turn him into a stone block altogether. Let's try it again. You start writing again and then when I give the sign you're no longer boys, but thirty-five pillars of stone.'

We regard this taboo sign—the 'holy sign'—as one of our most important technical devices. If the children are drilled—and we use the term 'drilled' advisedly—to obey it then it is difficult to imagine situations with which the teacher cannot instantly deal. This technical device makes him master of the situation at any given moment. It is hardly necessary to explain to the expert just how important that is,

Think, for example, of a situation in which danger threatens: in the middle of a noisy break the classroom has to be emptied. Instead of trying to make his voice heard above the noise the teacher claps his hands twice and absolute silence falls at once. He can then make himself understood without further difficulty.

We regard this matter, the technicalization of discussion, as very important. All communal work, whether instructional, administrative or educational proper is impossible without it. Here and there in Germany attempts have been made to bring the children themselves to deal with one stage of such chaos. They have been successful, but, as teachers in such classes have told us, only after many weeks of effort, and even then only after the teacher has intervened to guide the effort. We think this is a wrong approach. As much as we stress the desirability that the work and administration of a class should be carried out by the class itself, we feel nevertheless that the teacher should, to save time if for no other reason, take the organization in hand until the basis is prepared on which the real work of the community can develop.

The smooth running of the lessons is conditional also on the proper preparation of everything necessary for them: blackboard, chalk, duster, books, exercise books, maps, models, tools, projectors and slides, in short, whatever apparatus is required. It is the business of the whole class to see that all these necessary preparations are carried out. If one child fails to have his things ready then that hinders only himself, but if the things required by the class as a whole for the lesson are not ready in time, then the work of the whole class suffers.

As far as possible the children themselves should be given charge of all the class requisites. This means the appointment of monitors. Once a class is well trained in self-government then the children can appoint their own monitors without difficulty. It is a very different matter when the system of self-government is new, or when it is particularly desired to stress the educational aspect in a class which is already trained in self-government.

Thirty-two ten-year-old boys come into the bottom class of the higher school. They do not as yet know each other very well, and the teacher knows none of them. Clearly such a class cannot yet function as a self-governing community. For instance, if a teacher wants a clean blackboard at the beginning of a lesson then he must with such a class act on his own initiative and appoint one of the boys as blackboard monitor. Either the boy he appoints does the job well, in which case the nascent self-governing community will confirm him in his office, or he does it badly, in which case first of all an opportunity arises of influencing all the children, and secondly, an opportunity of securing a new appointment through the community.

Perhaps a day or so after the appointment of the blackboard monitor the teacher writes something on the blackboard. Suddenly one boy calls out:

'Please, sir, I can't see properly.'

Teacher: 'I can believe that. This blackboard is grey and smeary.'

No. 18: 'The blackboard monitor hasn't done his job properly.'

Several at once: 'Give the job to somebody else.'

Teacher, after giving the taboo sign: 'There's no need to get excited. I don't reproach the blackboard monitor because he hasn't done his job properly yet, just as I don't reproach any of you for failing to do a thing properly first go. But the class is right: it can't go on like this. Perhaps it was my mistake for appointing a boy who doesn't take the job seriously enough. But I didn't know any of you then, and you didn't know each other very well either. Now the situation is rather different. However, even so, it's not so easy. First of all, we must think it over. Are you going to appoint a boy so that he can then think a lot of himself and go around saying: 'See, they elected me!' Are you going to appoint one boy so that all the others who aren't appointed are jealous of the one you do appoint? Or are you going to make a choice so that the blackboard will be clean in the future and we can do our work without hindrance? What you've got to consider is are you going to make an opportunity for jealousy and boasting or for work?'

No. 28: 'For work, of course.'

Teacher: 'If we do that then certainly all those will be disappointed who are thinking to themselves: 'Ah! here's an opportunity to push ourselves forward.'' Appointment to an office is made not in order that whoever is appointed can flatter himself, but in order that the community is well served. Now I don't want to ask which of you would like the office, because if only a few answer I should have to suppose that some of them had thought only of the chance of making themselves big and not of the office itself. So let us think carefully over the problem of who is really suitable as a blackboard monitor. Take your time.'

The short silence that follows serves first of all to calm down the excited children, and secondly to give the act of appointing a blackboard monitor a certain aura of solemnity and responsibility. The trick always works. The children are put into a mood in which they take the matter seriously. You can see the change in their inner attitude from the expression on their faces.

Teacher: 'Well, who would like to make a proposal?'

No. 9: 'I propose No. 11.'

Teacher: 'I find the suggestion a very good one. I, too, think that No. 11 would do the job well. I think you'll all agree with that. Let's put the matter to the test. Whoever is in agreement with the appointment of No. 11 put up his hand.'

The great majority of the children raise their hands.

Teacher: 'Fine. Now we have a new blackboard monitor. And we elected him ourselves.'

The reader will not have failed to observe that in this case the teacher exercised a strong suggestive influence on the class. There were several reasons for that. First of all, we are only at the beginning of our organic growth as a class and we cannot afford to risk losing valuable time over such a minor matter, and there is, as yet, no special time set apart for discussing such things. Secondly, we are anxious to bring the children to realize that to take office means to enjoy the confidence of the community. This experience would only have been weakened by a long and perhaps endless discussion—consider for example, that each child might easily have proposed a different candidate.

Here is a second example of organic growth: One rainy day a boy is late. When he comes into the classroom the teacher notices that his boots are very muddy. Whilst the boy is making his excuses for his lateness the teacher looks him over and then, with his eyes fixed on the boy's boots, says:

'Your boots are very dirty, but, after all, perhaps that doesn't matter much. Go to your place.'

This observation causes some surprise in the class and, in consequence, the following conversation takes place:

Teacher: 'What are you looking so astonished about, No. 31?'

No. 31: 'Because you said dirty boots didn't matter much.'

Teacher: 'Well, do they?'

No. 4: 'When the mud dries you get dust.'

Teacher: 'That's right, but does that matter much?'

No. 32: 'Mud is dirt, and there are germs in dirt.'

E   65

In the further course of the discussion the children are brought to realize that it is not a matter of indifference what the individual does. If a boy has muddy boots it is not merely his affair, but the affair of all the others as well. For the first time they have some experience of the fact that there is no *res privata*. They then suggest that the teacher should 'appoint' a monitor. The teacher refuses. In the next lesson they propose that someone should be elected monitor. In answer to the teacher's inquiry as to why they hadn't made that proposal in the first place one of the boys replied naïvely: 'We didn't know we could do that. We thought that was only for the blackboard monitor.'

Thus all the various posts are filled, each at some particular opportunity. We wait until the necessity arises. We elect monitors only when circumstances arise which underline the necessity of the post in question. We regard this experience of the necessity of a thing as absolutely necessary, and it is impossible to exaggerate its importance. It is not a question of an organization thought out in all its details in the quiet of a master's study, but a question of organic development out of the need of the community.

Now let us see how the institution of a weekly discussion hour also developed organically. Under the influence of the new school the attitude of the children in this class during the breaks was unexceptionable for about a week. In the middle of the second week at school a nasty fight took place between two of the boys. They were separated and brought to book. The quarrel had arisen for trivial reasons. The inquiry into the matter was deliberately prolonged.

Teacher: 'Now all that took up twelve minutes of our time.'

No. 16: 'We lost all that time!'

No. 23: 'No. 32 is always starting a quarrel. He's strong and he hits the weaker boys.'

No. 32: 'That isn't true!'

All the children in an outburst: 'It is true! It is true!'

Teacher (calming the storm): 'I don't think we shall get much further that way. I'll give you a piece of advice. Think over why boys quarrel. I saw a boy just now shake his fist at No. 32. What do you think about that?'

No. 12: 'He meant, "You wait till we get you outside!" '

No. 16: 'He's going to punch him on the nose.'

No. 9: 'That means another fight, and so it goes on. That sort of thing won't do.'

No. 10: 'Someone or other must give way.'

Teacher: 'That's rather clever, but *I* think the squabblers know that just as well as you do, and still neither of them gives way.'

No. 5: 'They want to show how strong they are.'

No. 16: 'No. 32 is wild because he did so badly at sums today. He got everything wrong and the others all laughed at him.'

Teacher: 'You mean in multiplication? That happened to me when I was his age. But then a school-friend showed me how and after that I could do it. It often happens that a boy doesn't understand a thing like that immediately.'

No. 32, who has been sprawling defiantly in his place all the time, now pulls himself together and sits up.

Teacher: 'I wonder if one of you would be friendly enough to show No. 32 in the break how it's done.'

Many children volunteer.

Teacher: 'If you like, No. 32, you can choose which boy you want to help you. And now, boys, two of you were late again today and that disturbed us. And then the inkwells weren't filled, and that delayed us, too. I must talk to you about that.'

No. 11: 'No. 3 comes late almost every day.'

One of the boys makes a very disagreeable face and a contemptuous gesture. The teacher has been waiting for that for some time.

Teacher: 'No. 16, why are you making such a disagreeable face?'

No. 16: 'Because we aren't starting.'

Teacher: 'You're right. It's already half-past ten. But we just have to talk about such things. I can well believe that you would sooner continue our talk about how wells are made, but we have to talk about such things as being late. When are we going to do it?'

No. 5: 'Can't we stay behind afterwards?'

No. 2: 'If we did that my father would think I'd been kept in.'

Teacher: 'No. 5 didn't mean that we should stay behind every day. Perhaps once a week.'

No. 5: 'Lessons end on Saturdays at twelve o'clock. We could stay behind and talk about such things then.'

Teacher: 'Are you all in agreement that we should stay behind for a while on Saturdays to discuss things?'

General agreement.

Teacher: 'Then tell all your parents that from now on we are going to have a class discussion on Saturdays.'

Once again necessity leads to organization. That is organic growth.

Organizing the Lessons

By setting aside a special time for the discussion of administrative technical affairs the time for lessons can be fully utilized. From now on we shall have to use valuable lesson time for such matters only in really exceptional cases.

CHAPTER V

Self Government in Schools

The self-governing community sets its standards for all the offices it creates. Various children are appointed to be monitors and the monitors are kept under constant supervision by the community, which has a very keen eye for the merits and defects of those it has appointed.

It is much more difficult to set up standards where social problems are concerned, that is to say where the community is not giving guiding instructions to a particular monitor, but is laying down 'laws' for its own conduct. In setting such standards it is not a question of giving responsibility to an individual and supervising his activities, but the community takes the responsibility itself and exercises, if necessary, control over itself. Our experience has shown that very often the discussions of the self-governing community become unsatisfactory when there is a prospect of setting up a standard of this kind binding on all the members of the community. Resistance then arises, though the children are not always conscious of it. The discussion begins to flag and finally stops altogether or the children desperately try to divert it into other channels.

This strange phenomenon arises again and again and it has contributed more than a little to the condemnation of school self-government on the grounds either that the problems go beyond the understanding of the children or that their ethical feelings are not sufficiently mature to cope with them—and sometimes on the grounds that allegedly the children themselves reject self-government and prefer to be ruled by the firm hand of the teacher. We do not accept any of these reasons as valid. The attitude of the children is easily understandable in the light of Individual Psychology. The setting up of standards with a view to creating a real and vital community must unfavourably affect all children whose community feelings are inadequately developed and must therefore inevitably arouse their resistance. Individual Psychology is well acquainted with such 'resistances' from its experience in dealing with problem children, and even more so in its therapy for dealing with neurotic cases. It is therefore not thrown off its balance when it comes up against this resistance, and it is not in the least inclined to throw in its hand on that account.

The following ways of overcoming the resistance can be recommended:

1. Let the children divert the discussion into other channels if they want to, and then provoke the raising of the same theme again on another occasion. In our experience, the formulation and the adoption of a 'law' of a social nature will often come about without difficulty when the matter arises again out of some necessity. This method might be called the device of postponement.

2. Transfer the discussion of the subject and the formulation of the 'law', but not its adoption, to a smaller committee elected by the children themselves. This is the old device of dividing to conquer.

3. Provoke the self-respect of the community by saying something like: 'Very well, if there's no alternative I shall find a way out myself. It is, of course, a difficult problem and I'm not really surprised that you're falling more and more silent because you can't think of anything. I suppose I'm really asking too much of you. Do you want me to tell you, or would you prefer to wait until you get a bit older and find the solution for yourselves?' It is almost 90 per cent certain that this device of provoking the self-respect of the community will encourage the children to overcome their inner resistance, to tackle the problem again with renewed zeal and to find a suitable solution. If none of these methods proves successful then there is still a fourth possibility.

4. The teacher can take a tighter control over the discussion and lead the children to a solution by putting questions which narrow down the possibilities. This is the device of helpful intervention, and it will often be found necessary.

5. If two teachers are taking part in the discussion, then, if the class falls obstinately silent, they can continue the discussion in an artificial duel. Of course, the preliminary condition for the success of this method is that the second teacher should have grasped the intention of the leader of the discussion and that he should co-operate in

bringing it to fruition. This game of ball between the two teachers can go on until either a child puts in a word, or until a suitable moment arrives when one teacher can say to the other: 'Don't you think that one or the other of the children might give his opinion now?' In this way, the continued co-operation of the class in the debate is encouraged. We can call this device 'the ball-game'.

6. Or the teachers can lay bare the real reasons for the inner resistance of the children, and that can be done in two ways. First of all indirectly: one teacher can turn to the other saying, 'It seems to me that the class doesn't want to take part any more. Suddenly everyone has fallen silent. That reminds me of what once happened to me when I was a boy. My father was talking to me about how nice it is if one person helps another. We talked about how that went on in the factories. I mentioned a number of examples to my father and went on chatting away eagerly. And then suddenly my father said: "And what about helping your mother? How do you think you could best do that?" I said something or other and went on talking, but really my joy in the discussion was gone. As long as I was laying down the law for other people to obey I was very enthusiastic about it all. But when it looked as though the law was going to put me to inconvenience . . . ah, that was a different matter! I said to myself at the time: "Speech is silver; silence is golden." And I think our lads here prefer gold to silver.'

Or the teacher can lay bare the reasons directly, saying: 'Really, of course, I can quite understand why you have all fallen so silent. You realize quite clearly: if we make a law now we shall have to obey it; if we lay down what we think ought to be then we shall have no alternative but to carry it out. That, of course, won't be easy; it will be difficult and it won't be pleasant. And then a voice inside you says: "Very well, don't lay down what ought to be and then you won't have to carry it out. Don't make a law at all and then you won't have to keep it." But that's acting like the ostriches. When the ostrich sees danger coming it buries its head in the sand. Then it can't see the danger and so it believes that the danger isn't there any more. The danger for you now is the inconvenience such a law might cause you. And when you fall silent you are like the ostrich who buries his head in the sand. But what ought to be is still right even if you don't say it.'

When we talk of setting up standards or adopting laws the question arises: in what form is this to take place? Differences of opinion on this point have produced a voluminous literature. Many people are in favour of clearly formulated laws which should be written down so that the community can refer to them in case of need. In other words, the codification of class laws. But the difficulty here is—and whoever has had any practical teaching experience will certainly agree with us —that the cases in which the conduct of children has to be referred to a desirable standard are so many and so varied that even a codification which went into the minutest details could never hope to cover everything that arises in the manifold relationships between the children themselves and between them and their teachers. And further, in our experience many children set themselves out to find gaps in the class laws. And when they have succeeded they announce triumphantly: 'There is nothing against it in the laws of our class!' We must try to avoid any division of the class community into two camps, with the good sheep on one side, and the black sheep on the other, always on the look-out for some gap in the entanglement of regulations and prohibitions, through which they can crawl successfully, thumbing their noses at the law and the law-givers and dancing with delight when they succeed.

The setting up of laws is nothing more than the establishment of social defence by extraneous means. But that in itself—as a glance at the world of grown-ups is quite enough to convince us—is by no means enough. There is truly no lack of rules and regulations in the world, but what is so often lacking is inner approval of the law. Here for the first time our critical eye is directed to a real chink in the theory that school self-government means primarily that the children themselves formulate laws to govern their own conduct. A law adopted by the community itself rather than one imposed on it from without is not likely to be more respected on that account. In our experience we have come across children who pursue law-breakers with a keen eye and understanding, who ruthlessly expose the logic chopping of the offenders, and who propose water-tight texts—and who then violate the very laws they have themselves demanded and formulated. Such experiences are calculated to make us modest in our expectations. We must not concentrate on the suppression of improprieties and indiscipline by extraneous regulations, but instead we must encourage the children to become aware of moral standards, and bring them to an inner approval of the law.

It will already have become clear that the framework of the class as a mere legislative self-governing community is too narrow, and an examination of the institution which plays the main role in most systems of school self-government, namely the children's courts, will confirm this.

Once a class or school community has set up certain standards by legislative act, the carrying out of its provisions is entrusted to a special category of officials elected by the community. With this, the power to punish is placed in the hands of children, though almost always there is a court of appeal in the shape of the teacher, the teaching body or the headmaster. It is probably very rare nowadays that the power to punish is placed in the hands of individual children. Those educators who advocate the establishment of children's courts —later on we shall see why they necessarily demand such courts— generally propose that minor offences should be dealt with by a bench of judges, whilst more serious offences should be dealt with by the class or school community. As we have already mentioned, a condemned accused has the right of appeal. Public judicial institutions are often copied so closely in these courts that prosecutors, defending counsel and juries are appointed, but generally speaking, prosecution and defence take place in the form of free discussion.

But educators adopting this system find it even more troublesome to decide on the kind of punishment to be imposed than they do to appoint judicial officials and decide the method of court procedure. Innumerable proposals have been made in this respect. To give an example of a point of view which is almost certainly near the golden mean let us quote the attitude of Dr. Wilhelm Mann as laid down in his book *Schulstaat und Selbstregierung der Schuler*. (We have italicized the passages which we regard as of particular interest):

'The only offences which should be brought before the children's forum are those which violate the regulations of the system of self-government itself. *Where offences of a more serious nature are involved it will be found impossible to dispense with the judicial intervention of the teacher.* At the outside, the judicial officials of the children themselves may be drawn into the consideration of such matters with an advisory voice, as Professor Heckmann has done in Elberfeld. *There are cases in which children cannot be expected to show a proper understanding for the offence. A proper understanding presupposes psychological insight and a consideration of individual factors, and this is not always possible where children of the same age as the accused are concerned.*

'Secondly, the children's court must be competent with regard to the punishments it imposes. For this reason it must limit itself essentially to punishments which are placed in the hands of the children by the system of self-government. Such punishments are, on the one hand: a rebuke before the officials of the class or before the class itself with a corresponding note in the records and, on the other hand, the suspension of rights such as *the loss of the right to vote, the loss of the right to speak at class meetings, or the loss of the right to take part in the system of self-government at all, and further, expulsion from intercourse with the other children, and, finally, removal from an official post.* In addition, one can also impose without misgivings certain "natural" punishments, such as having to arrive before lessons begin in the case of repeated unpunctuality, or cleaning work in cases of lack of cleanliness. Some of these punishments can be imposed conditionally, for instance, in the event of subsequent improvement, the term of the punishment imposed can be reduced.

'Children are quite capable of judging the degree and nature of such punishments and their extent. *It is quite a different matter with other punishments involving work or the loss of freedom—teachers themselves even impose such punishments in very uneducational fashion.*

'The children's court may impose the following punishments:

'The administration of a rebuke before the class court or before the class meeting with a corresponding note in the register:

'Cleaning work such as the collection of paper in the school and the schoolyards. This punishment may be imposed only where the offence has been against cleanliness and tidiness.

'*Punishment for coming late* can be to make the offender report in the classroom half an hour before the beginning of the lesson.'

Moderate as are the views expressed in the quotation, they still do not quite accord with our own experience. The last-named punishment, that for late-coming, is particularly suited as a jumping-off ground to illustrate the educational inadequacy of the collective punishment system. But we must ask our readers to exercise a little patience because, first of all, we must pause to examine the problem of late-coming itself in the light of Individual Psychology.

Let us consider, first of all, what we have already said about the processes of the human mind. There are many adults who find a visit to the dentist so disagreeable that they cannot easily make up their minds to carry it out. When the necessity arises they adopt all sorts of transparent tricks in order to postpone the disagreeable moment. They find, for example, that they 'just haven't time to fit it in'. Unimportant matters, which might well be postponed to some

74

other time, begin to take on the character of important affairs demanding immediate attention. Such people suddenly show much more zeal for their work; they leave the office later than usual; they have urgent matters to attend to; and they find that there are jobs they have to do which they have long postponed but which now call urgently for settlement—in short, they 'just have no time to go to the dentist'. And they fail to realize that they themselves are doing everything possible precisely in order to have no time. They are doing everything they can to evade a disagreeable necessity, but at the same time they like to regard their pseudo-reasons as real and thus flatter their own vanity: 'Am I really a coward? Oh no! It's not that; it's just that I have no time. When once I've settled all these urgent matters. . . .'

We see that the human mind is very clever at inventing excuses which can really stand superficial examination. Late-coming on the part of children is in the same category; it is an arrangement on the part of the child's mind to avoid or postpone something unpleasant. Of course, there are often very good reasons why a child is late for school. If a child has to travel by some public conveyance, then it really will sometimes happen that he is delayed by a traffic jam, or something of the sort. But where repeated lateness is concerned it is quite a different matter. In this case there is certainly some arrangement at work of which the child is not actively aware and it is just like the arrangement by which the adult who is afraid of visiting his dentist provides himself with sham reasons for not going. There are a great variety of sham reasons for being constantly late at school, but only one real reason, and that is an inner resistance against going to school. In most cases the child is not actively aware of this inner resistance or the arrangement.

Edgar has been egged on by his mother into an exaggerated ambition. If a mistake or failing on his part is publicly noted by the teacher, the result is tears. A class note which is not up to standard makes him positively ill. His mother reports: 'It so upsets him that he vomits, looks dreadful and trembles.' It appears that this state of excessive nerves usually occurs just before it is time for him to go off to school. The result is that every week he is late two or three times. This goes on until in the end Edgar's lateness becomes a permanent phenomenon. Is Edgar now to be placed before a class court? No responsible person could agree. They would all say, 'But the child is ill and therefore he must be excused.'

Eric has a younger sister of whom he is exceedingly jealous. He has farther to go to school than she has and therefore he must leave the house earlier. In addition, the mother takes the sister to school. The jealous Eric thinks to himself: 'Why does mother always take her to school? Why does she never take me to school?' He begins to wait behind secretly to observe the two as they go off to school. 'Perhaps mother buys her something I don't know anything about!' Day after day he does his shadowing with the result that he is constantly late for school. In the end the mother learns about his frequent lateness. There is a disagreeable scene, and after that Eric is punctual again for a while. But then he starts his spying again. The teacher again informs the mother and there is another scene. This does not help either; Eric continues to come late. Is Eric to be placed before a class court? Eric isn't ill. He doesn't vomit; he doesn't look dreadful; he doesn't tremble. And yet: he is a child with a deadly fear in his heart, the fear that he is coming too short in the affections of his mother, and this oppresses and upsets him. If the community now punishes him for his late-coming and he feels misunderstood then his isolation will be intensified.

At this point someone may object that these are exceptional cases, and that there are many children who are constantly late at school merely because they are lazy and won't take the trouble to be on time. But whoever makes this objection is confusing the symptom with the sickness itself. He is supposing that one symptom of discouragement—evasion by late-coming—is caused by another, namely laziness and the refusal to take the trouble to be in time. But laziness and the refusal to bother are themselves nothing but terms which represent a summary description of a certain line of conduct. Instead of saying: 'The boy doesn't learn the essentials; he just copies his work; he does things by halves or not at all; he takes no part in the discussion,' and so on, the teacher just says: 'The boy is lazy.' Now in some cases late-coming belongs to this laziness, and in others a strange slowing down of physical movement. If only teachers would at last realize that a word like 'laziness' neither explains an attitude nor helps towards its understanding! We can 'understand' laziness only if we trace back the attitude to the thing that conditions it; if we look behind the apparent passivity of the child and see the activity, which is expended in an avoidance of the tasks life imposes on him, an activity which takes the form of laziness; if we realize that laziness is not a passive attitude, but an active one of which the child is not consciously aware. It is something that may be compared to the 'action' of a neurotic, who, like the lazy boy, is not actively aware of his attempt to evade tasks he believes himself unable to perform, or of the 'arrangements' he is making to effect this. It is discouragement which drives them all—the lazy boys, the late-comers and the rest—to desert from the school front. Laziness as a motive for late-coming! This term, which beclouds the whole wide sphere of education, disappears in the searchlight of Individual Psychology.

Let us now place such a deserter before a class court. Let him be condemned to appear in the classroom even earlier than the time for the lesson. It may well be, of course, that the child finds the punishment so disagreeable that in future he is no longer late for class. But has his inner evasion really been liquidated? It may even be that by his enforced presence the child is enabled to do his work better, thereby attaining a success experience which increases his courage and persuades him to abandon his evasions. So in this case the punishment has achieved the desired effect, and the triumph of the advocates of the punishment system is complete. Not so fast! In a certain percentage of cases such outward success is undoubtedly obtained. After all, who would persist in a method which never proved successful even in appearance? But should we leave it to chance to decide whether a child proceeds on his own to dismantle such an evasive arrangement? That is the crux of the matter. Individual Psychology is convinced, from hundreds of such experiences, that a teacher can do much more, and, in particular, that he can help to bring about *the desired inner change in the child.*

Our knowledge of the human mind has taught us that this inner change—which is nothing more or less than the acceptance by the child of the rules of the community—takes place only when the child realizes the fundamental error which has led it to the useless side of life, and adopts the positive aim presented to it. Here is the parting of the ways. Whoever is really serious about education cannot be satisfied by mere legislation designed to secure the smooth working of the school and by the punishment of those children who offend against the law. He cannot confine himself to dealing with mere outward symptons, and he must strive to discover the real motives of children who break the law. He must lay bare the error of their ways so that he can deal with the evil where it really lies. Whoever is really serious about education cannot be satisfied with superficial methods; he will soon find himself squarely faced with the necessity of using

77

the more profound educational methods provided by Individual Psychology on the basis of its long, practical experience.

When teachers who regarded the school as a place of education introduced self-government and turned the class into a legislative assembly, that was a great step forward. Repeated violations of the law then made the introduction of school courts a necessity, because in the absence of profounder methods to bring the offenders to heel, they were compelled to exert such pressure. But we can see that the educational effectiveness of all these systems of school self-government is limited. So long as self-government in the schools is confined to the narrow limits of legislation, bureaucracy and school courts it can certainly give many opportunities for individual children to alter their style of life, it can even influence such individual children with superficial methods, but it cannot get at forces operating within the child of which the child itself is not actively aware; it cannot touch that secret life style of the child which actually determines its whole attitude.

The position would be very different if the community did more than merely condemn anti-social behaviour and went on to discover and reveal its motives; to recognize the error which holds the problem child a prisoner without his conscious knowledge; to lay bare the peculiar dynamics which drive the child into the world of fantasy away from the world of reality. How very different the situation would be if the class community adopted the attitude of the understanding helper rather than that of the judge!

Such a change would give a new objective to the whole system of self-government in the schools, an objective which distinguishes the system of Individual Psychology from all others. But that objective can be accepted only by those who realize that community means more than the setting up of rules and regulations and the condemnation and punishment of the individual who fails to obey them; only by those who, conscious of their own imperfections, regard the offender as misguided, as so burdened by his discouragement that he is *unable* to perform the tasks life imposes on him, do everything possible to help him. We must take Dr. Adler's wise advice to heart: 'Those who stumble should not be trampled on but helped to their feet.'

When we now approach the problem of self-government in the schools from the angle of this new objective we shall appreciate that the object of the class as a legislative community is not so much to lay down the law as to bring the children to a realization that certain standards of conduct are necessary. Perhaps we can best illustrate this with an example.[1]

Teacher: 'We have decided to hold the class discussion in two parts: on conduct and on progress.'

Pupil 24: 'Let's take progress first.'

Teacher: 'I can imagine why some of you would sooner talk about your progress today. They are probably afraid to hear some unpleasant things.'

Pupil 19: 'Today at eleven o'clock there was a great deal of disturbance in the break. It was unworthy of a class in the Upper School.'

Teacher: 'Let the boys tell us why there was so much disturbance today.'

Pupil 9: 'Perhaps they were still excited from Sunday.'

Pupil 6: 'Perhaps some of them saw a Wild-West film at the pictures yesterday.'

Pupil 19: 'Sometimes a boy's out for a lark and then he teases the others.'

Pupil 2: 'Let the boys who were responsible give their own reasons.'

Pupil 9: 'Perhaps some of them got tired of sitting. We have to sit down too much.'

Teacher: 'No. 9 is right. Like most other schools, our school isn't built as it ought to be. We have no playground and therefore we have to stay in the classrooms during breaks.'

Pupil 27: 'The classroom is too small for so many boys.'

Teacher: 'That raises a problem. How would I, as in charge of the class, stand to the problem of the break if we had a playground?'

Pupil 18: 'You would be afraid that something would happen, because you would be made responsible for it.'

Teacher: 'But there's just as much danger that something might happen in the classroom.'

Pupil 21: 'Something could happen in the playground and then the teacher would have to take the blame.'

Pupil 20: 'The responsibility is still greater in the classroom.'

Teacher: 'And so is the danger. Why are we talking about all this?'

Pupil 27: 'You want us to realize just what the situation is.'

Teacher: 'Why can running around be permitted in a playground and not in a classroom?'

[1] Taken from Dr. St. Maday's translation in *A Jovo Utjain*, Budapest.

Pupil 6: 'In a playground there is grass and there's not so much danger.'

Pupil 20: 'In the playground it's just an accident if anything happens. Inside anything can happen any moment.'

Pupil 27: 'It's easy to hurt yourself in the classroom; there are edges and corners everywhere.'

Teacher: 'There is more chance that a boy will hurt himself in the classroom.'

Pupil 18: 'Accidents can happen anywhere.'

Teacher: 'I should like to hear the opinions of others.'

Pupil 25: 'What's the use of talking about a playground when we haven't got one?'

Pupil 18: 'But perhaps we could get one.'

Pupil 21: 'We have discussed what we should do if we had a playground. Now we must discuss what we have to do because we haven't got one.'

Pupil 23: 'The breaks are so short that it wouldn't be worth while to go out into a playground. A teacher would have to be in the playground all the time.'

Pupil 19: 'Instead of four breaks we could have three longer ones.'

Teacher: 'The discussion has now got to the point where I can say something: we have discussed how it would be if we had a playground, and we have come to the conclusion as indicated by one boy; that it's a matter of necessity—the teacher doesn't want to make life difficult for you. It is, after all, a very different thing if we have to stay in the classroom and have no playground.'

Pupil 27: 'We haven't got so much room in our classroom and therefore we mustn't behave ourselves so wildly. The discussion has shown us that teachers aren't out to cramp us.'

Pupil 21: 'What Pupil 28 has said really means that we must control ourselves more.'

As the reader can see, the class has not formulated another law, but come to a new realization of facts. We know perfectly well, of course, that a realization of something is not the same thing as appropriate action based on the realization, but we will discuss that later. First of all, let us take another example calculated to show the fundamental difference between formulating regulations and winning through to a realization of facts. As whoever wrote down the record omitted the names of the speakers we shall refer to whichever child is speaking simply as X.

Pupil 3: 'Let's talk about the increasing roughness in the class.'

Teacher: 'Yes, it's true, some of you go a bit too far, pommel each other, and so on.'

(Some of the children laugh.)

Teacher (turning to second teacher): 'Did you notice that quite a lot of boys did not join in the laughter? Some of them are more serious than one might expect at their age.'

Teacher No. 2 (turning to several of the children who are looking at him in a perplexed fashion): 'Perhaps you think we are talking in riddles.'

(The class has now become quiet and serious.)

Teacher No. 1: 'Can we begin now?'

X: 'There's a boy here who's always egging on others to say something, but the result is that they feel less inclination than ever to say anything.'

Teacher No. 2: 'Well, will you make the boy in question realize that he is not being very helpful? You could do it better than anyone else, I think.'

(Pupil 3 and the boy sitting behind him both get to their feet at once. Several of the boys call out 'Ssssh!' Pupil 3 looks round, sees that the boy behind him is standing, and sits down again.)

Teacher: 'I think some of you have noticed what I noticed. (A boy wants to speak.) I'm glad that you've got such sharp eyes.'

X: 'I think the pommelling starts off with insults. The weaker boys insult the stronger boys and then there's a fight.'

Teacher No. 2: 'So only the stronger boys may pommel?'

X: 'No. That wouldn't be a class community.'

X: 'Fist rule holds good in our class.'

X: 'Perhaps we are going through a rowdy period.'

Teacher No. 2: 'And are we to fold our arms and wait until the rowdy period is over? Perhaps there are some boys here who would like to persuade us that rowdiness is necessary and ought to be encouraged. I'm not against rowdiness. It's not a tragedy.'

(Here Teacher No. 2 is using the device of identifying himself with the interest of the boys. He seems to take their side.)

Teacher No. 1: 'I quite agree. But as nature has given us brains to think with perhaps we can go into the matter a bit further.'

Teacher No. 2: 'Perhaps there are arguments on the other side as well.'

X: 'It isn't the strongest boys who go in for the pommelling in our

F   81

class; it's those who can't do anything anyhow, who are the rowdiest.'

X: 'A boy who wants a fight will only attack another rowdy. If he pushes a boy over who he knows will only get up again and not hit back there's no fun in that. The rowdy wants a fight, and it takes two to make a fight.'

Teacher No. 1 writes on the blackboard: 'It takes two to make a fight.'

At this point there is a gap in the record.

X: 'Why does no one strike No. 3?'

X: 'Because they all know that No. 3 won't hit back, and there's no fun in that.'

X: 'No. 3 isn't a rowdy.'

Teacher No. 2: 'And is there anything else to be said about No. 3?'

(Silence in the class.)

Teacher No. 2: 'It seems to me that you are all hesitating to draw a conclusion here because you are afraid it might be disagreeable for you.'

(An even longer silence.)

X: 'No. 3 is a serious boy.'

X: 'No. 3 is an intelligent boy.'

Teacher No. 1: 'When one of the rowdies thinks of No. 3 he probably feels something or the other.'

X: 'Crassus was stronger, but Caesar was the greater thinker.'

(The class had just been through the period of the Caesars in their history lessons.)

Teacher No. 2: 'Well, there's not much danger in talking about a situation which existed two thousand years ago. Perhaps some of you think it's so difficult to be a Caesar that it isn't worth trying.'

Teacher No. 1: 'Now the time has come to look into yourselves. What do you think of a boy like No. 3 who doesn't hit back when he is attacked?'

X: 'If a boy isn't any good in class he tries to distinguish himself by being a rowdy outside.'

X: 'There are two sorts of victories: one you win with brawn and the other with brains.'

Teacher No. 2: 'Think of a man like Gandhi: he just stands there and makes no resistance to anything that is done to him.'

X: 'He doesn't do anything to become famous: he just becomes famous.'

Self Government in Schools

X: 'The world has veneration for Gandhi and we have respect for No. 3.'

(Teacher No. 1 writes up on the blackboard: 'Respect, veneration, admiration.')

X: 'We admire No. 3. Now he can stick his chest out.'

Teacher No. 1: 'I rather think he'll be content with the respect. He is quite intelligent enough. He doesn't want admiration. And if you admire him it won't hurt him because he doesn't want to be admired. He is satisfied with being respected.'

X: 'He's an example to the rest of us.'

(The class discussion is over. Several of the boys pounce on No. 3 and pommel him in a friendly fashion. In reality they would sooner have embraced him.)

Once again the class has refrained from formulating any law. There has been no vote and no threat of sanctions: 'Whoever breaks our decision against rowdiness will be punished by. . . .' On the contrary, our discussion concerned itself with the motives that impel children to a line of conduct that disturbs the community; it rejected the negative aim and adopted the positive aim instead. The boy who spoke of Crassus and Caesar may well have won through to a first general idea of the primacy of mind over matter. His formulation: 'There are two sorts of victories: one you win with brawn and the other with brains' is quite along the general line of Individual Psychology. In boyish language it expresses what Individual Psychology describes as the useful and the useless sides of life. And the same applies to the remark: 'If a boy isn't any good in class he tries to distinguish himself by being a rowdy outside.' These boys have no idea of the processes of the human mind, and yet they can see through quite a lot of things. 'Out of the mouths of babes and sucklings. . . .' Again and again we have found that if children are taken seriously and encouraged to think for themselves they often come to results which would not shame an adult mind. Of course, the attitude of the child must be directed constantly towards the community; an isolated child left to itself would never arrive at such conclusions, but in the community one idea naturally leads to another.

It should be clear to the reader by now that self-government in the schools according to the system of Individual Psychology goes very much farther than the usual system of legislative, administrative and judicial functions.

83

CHAPTER VI

Monitors, Leaders and Helpers

☆

S hould a monitor become neglectful and do his job badly he is called to account by the community. Sometimes the annoyance of the class expresses itself vehemently, and then there is often demand for the culprit's dismissal. When that happens the situation is a difficult one from the educational point of view. On the one hand, the community is undoubtedly in the right when it demands that its affairs should be managed properly by those it has appointed to manage them, and such a call for dismissal must therefore be taken seriously. On the other hand, it must not be forgotten that the monitor sees things through his own particular glasses. And that is a point that should never be forgotten. His failings do not bulk large in his own eyes, and he does not regard the demand for his dismissal as entirely objective. To him it sounds more like: 'Crucify him!' 'Down with him!' And he feels that the root of it is envy. He is not entirely in the wrong in so thinking. Children are, after all, all more or less egoistic. If they were not it would not be necessary to educate them so carefully in a community spirit. Now the demand for dismissal can also involve the danger of a split in the class, because the monitor will probably have his friends, and they will support him. Personalities then enter into the argument. Boy stands against boy. Group against group. It is certainly a difficult situation, but there are a number of ways in which it can be met.

 1. The method of postponement. The teacher gives the taboo sign. 'Stop. You are all much too excited. We must postpone the discussion to another time when all of you are calmer and able to see that the thing doesn't call for a revolution. Until then it's best to leave things as they are.'

postpone
discussion

2. The method of arbitration. Teacher: 'When the oven's too hot

the joint gets burnt. Let us hand over this difficult case to a commission for discussion. The monitor will appoint his representative; the class will appoint its representative, and I will appoint mine. These three lads can then discuss the matter and work out practical proposals.'

3. The method of the helping hand. Teacher: 'I have a feeling that it really is rather difficult to carry out this job satisfactorily. The monitor has not only his office to think of, but other things as well, just as you all have. How would it be if we appointed someone to assist him? Two heads are better than one, and two pairs of hands can do more than one.' The appointment of an assistant monitor will often mean that the assistant takes over the office progressively until finally the unsatisfactory monitor is painlessly removed.

4. The method of irony. Teacher: 'I think just to dismiss him is much too namby-pamby. Why not sentence him to be hanged, drawn and quartered? There would be no difficulty about finding the executioners, I'm sure. I can already see quite a number of willing boys.' Or: 'To dismiss or not to dismiss; that is the question. And what a question! No wonder you're all so excited. But just consider: you don't crack a nut with a steam-hammer.'

5. The method of objectivity. Teacher: 'Both sides in the discussion seem very worked up about it all. The one side sees that the office has been neglected and, up to a point, it is right. The monitor sees not so much his own failings as the fact that quite a number of the other boys envy him his job. And up to a point he is right, too. Thus we see that both sides are not altogether wrong. But, at the same time, both sides are not altogether right. Perhaps there is some satisfactory middle path? But it can be found only by someone who is mentally mature enough to be able to separate personalities from the matter at stake.' (The teacher turns to the blackboard and writes up: 'Personality: object.') 'The personality, that is, the monitor himself; the object, that is, his office. The one who finds the middle path can't be a boy who decides according to his feelings: "If he's my friend I'm on his side; if he's not my friend I'm against him," but a boy who says to himself: "If he does his job properly then I'm on his side; if he doesn't, then I'm against him." '

6. The method of identification. Teacher: 'It's not difficult to turn against a boy who has made a mistake, and there isn't much credit to be gained out of it. Now there has been a mistake in this case, as we all know. You know it and I know it. It's much more difficult to

think: "Now how should I stand if I were in his shoes? If I found so many of the boys against me?" It's difficult to put yourself in some- one else's shoes, very difficult, and I can quite understand that not all of you are capable of doing it. But those who do succeed in doing it will avoid every word which might hurt.'

7. The 'Golden Bridge' method. Teacher: 'It seems to me quite unnecessary that you should work yourselves up as much as some of you are doing. When I look at our monitor I have a feeling that he isn't enjoying his job much any more and that he's quite prepared to resign. I may be mistaken, of course, but that's my impression. And perhaps, if I were in his place, I should feel much the same when I saw such a tremendous to-do being made out of a minor error.'

Which of these methods is actually used will depend, of course, entirely on the nature of the case and on the given situation. One or the other of them will be used when there is a danger that sharp antagonism will develop in the class. So long as the class shows that it can discuss the matter at issue objectively then there is no need for the teacher to exert any specially strong influence.

But even in this more favourable case the teacher must still have a trick or two up his sleeve because whether it is really a question of a voluntary resignation or a pseudo-voluntary one, or one that is im- posed by the class, there is always the possibility that the boy in question feels that he has suffered a defeat and thus the danger of discouragement, and it is this danger which we must do our best to obviate.

To achieve this we bring about a discussion with the boy in ques- tion. We don't obviously encourage him and we don't 'console' him in the ordinarily understood fashion, but we do use one or the other, according to the nature of the case, of our various little tricks which are calculated to make the defeat tolerable, to raise the depressed self-confidence, to prevent the rise of a feeling hostile to the com- munity which has brought about the defeat, and to allow the boy to extract permanent advantage for his own spiritual attitude from his defeat. This is also a good opportunity to show the difference between Individual Psychological methods and the ordinary, everyday methods in use. It is a great temptation to burden a child with the consequences of its own wrong attitude and then leave him to get on with it as best he can. If he succeeds, good; if he fails, the further responsibility for his failure can then be added. This sort of attitude is frequently expressed in the words: 'It serves you right. The next time you'll have more sense and act differently.' It reveals a truly frightening lack of educational understanding. The whole point at issue is precisely how the child understands his experience from his own point of view. Because in similar circumstances an adult would think: 'All right. Next time I'll have more sense and do it differently', does it follow that the child reacts in the same way? The child does not necessarily see things as an adult does. Precisely in the case with which we are dealing the main thing is to try to see the thing with the eyes of the child and to feel the experience inwardly as he feels it. And for this we shall have to use the little tricks we are about to list, modified according to the particular circumstances of the case. Here, of course, we can only generalize.

1. *Guidance.* This method can be used when the monitor complained of has not actually been deposed. Teacher: 'So we have decided to give you another trial. Now, of course, it's very easy just to say: "Mind you do it better in future!" But it's much more difficult to say just *how* you are to do it better in the future. Perhaps with the best will in the world, you don't quite know how to do it better. If that is the case, then despite all your good will you probably won't be able to do it much better. And therefore we must all of us come to some clear understanding as to just how your job should be done so that you will know yourself whether you're doing it properly or not.' (This is then followed by a discussion of how the thing should be done.)

2. *Consolation.* This method will be used when the boy has been deposed and he is upset in consequence. Teacher: 'Such things often happen in the world. You can't expect people to praise someone who doesn't do his job properly. Perhaps some of the boys have made more fuss than was absolutely necessary. In fact, I think some of them did. But it's not really a great affair of State, you know. There's really no need for you to get so excited about it. Everyone makes mistakes sometimes. I often have, I know. No one's finished for good and all just because he's made a mistake.' (This line is taken in order to deal with the immediate situation. Later on there will be a further treatment along Individual Psychological lines as indicated later.)

3. *Diversion.* This method should be used in cases where the boy really hasn't done the job properly and where the teacher sees any further attempt to carry on would endanger the boy's spiritual development. Teacher: 'To tell you the truth, I'm rather glad they

decided to remove you. And because I say that perhaps you're thinking now: "Oh, so even the teacher is against me!" Perhaps you may even think: "So he's on the side of those boys who went for me so unkindly!" Perhaps there's a little truth in that, but only a very little. I really am on the side of boys who think a job ought to be done properly, so that I am, as I said, really rather glad about it. Perhaps you think that's very unkind of me. But when I tell you why I am glad you'll see that I'm not your enemy after all. Caesar could write a letter, dictate a letter and read a letter all at the same time. Think of it! At the same time! But he was a great man. We can't all be great men. Most of us find it difficult to think of two things at once, never mind three. But that's just what you have been asked to do. You had to think not only about everything that concerns you as a member of the class, but also, and at the same time, about what concerned you as a monitor. Well, now you haven't got to think of the monitor's job—you'll have more time to think about what concerns you just as a member of the class. Now perhaps you begin to understand why I said I was glad? It's because you'll find it easier to do your work. Previously you were rather hampered because you had to be a monitor as well.'

4. *Change of Aim*. This method in particular shows us the difference between the usual, everyday sort of encouragement and consolation and the Individual Psychological method of laying things bare. Teacher: 'I can quite imagine how you see this matter. Perhaps if I were in your place I should see it in the same way as you do. In fact, it's very probable that I should. You feel terribly upset because your classmates have taken away your job. Perhaps you are already wondering how you can get your own back on this or that one of the boys who were against you. I can understand that quite well. But you admit that you did make mistakes. You say to yourself: "Yes, of course, it's quite true I didn't do everything as I ought to have done it, but it wasn't as bad as all that. They ought not to have taken away my job." That's how the matter looks from your point of view, and it makes you feel that you have been defeated, that you have fought a battle and lost it. And at the same time you are wondering how you can win the next battle. But isn't there perhaps another and a better way? Yes, there certainly is, but it isn't an easy one. In fact, it's very difficult and I'm not at all sure you'll be capable of taking it. I'll tell you what it is though, and then whether you do what I suggest or not will depend entirely on you. If I say, "You did

that well!" then you feel pleased and you make even greater efforts.
To do things properly—that is a victory in itself. Every victory makes
you stronger and determined to do it even better than ever, to rise
still higher. When you lost your job it was a defeat. Very well, now
comes the difficult part. Make use of your defeat. Do things better in
the future. Use your defeat to rise higher. Think to yourself: "So I
was careless, was I? Well, it's true. I was careless. But now I'm going
to learn from my defeat. From now on I'm going to set myself a new
aim: to be careful and tidy. I don't need to be a monitor for that. I
can do it on my own." And now where is the enemy? Is it your classmates who deposed you today? Even if they did show you your failings rather cruelly perhaps? Or is the enemy you must now defeat your
own carelessness? Think it over: who's the fellow to go for? The boy
who shouts "Fire!" at the top of his voice when the fire's there, or
the boy who started the fire? Your classmates shouted "Fire" today,
but not without cause. They've shown you that you're in danger of
becoming a boy with bad habits, carelessness. Perhaps there were one
or two of them who didn't care much about that and were really only
anxious to trip you up. Right, but think what they've done without
knowing it! They have helped you to set yourself a new aim: not ven-
geance on an imaginary enemy, but a real battle against a real enemy:
your own carelessness. I realize you won't find it easy to say to yourself: "Really I ought to thank them for this. Anybody can rise higher
on victories, but I am determined to learn from my own defeat and
to do things properly in the future." Now do you see what I meant
when I told you that the right way was the difficult way? But I think
you're the sort of boy who could take the difficult way if he once set
his mind to it.'

And now let us turn our attention to those boys who are not
monitors with an administrative job to do, but boys who have been
chosen class or group leaders and whose job is to influence the
behaviour of the class. Their job really is difficult.

The most important thing such a leader has to do is to see to it
that the behaviour of the individual members of the class before the
lessons or during the breaks is orderly. The class is divided up into a
number of groups, each of which consists of four or five children.
Each group elects a group leader. All the children of the class as a
whole elect a class leader. Different classes have their different ways
of doing these things, and it really does not matter much whether a
class elects only group leaders and not a class leader, or only a class

leader and not group leaders, or both. The spirit in which these various offices are carried out is much more important. Our long experience suggests that at first these leaders tend to regard their function as a supervisory one. They don the mantle of authority, start ordering their fellows around, and are then very surprised to find that they are not always obeyed. At this point they will undoubtedly come running to the teacher full of bitter complaints and demanding severe punishments for the boys who have refused to recognize their authority. The regularity with which this happens should not lead to a premature abandonment of the experiment of self-government, perhaps with the excuse: 'The children aren't ripe for self-government yet and they require firm handling by a teacher.' When the teacher refuses the demands of these leaders they will go off and carry on with their jobs for a while, but, almost invariably, they will return and tell the teacher they want to resign. Once again, this must not lead to an abandonment of the experiment, but should be utilized as a welcome opportunity to intervene in a truly educational fashion on the basis of the children's own experience. The leaders have seen in practice that the way in which they carry out their responsible job has led to no results. We therefore take the opportunity of calling a meeting of these leaders to discuss the situation and we encourage them to find out for themselves what mistakes they have made. As a result of their discussion they decide that in future they will adopt a far more friendly attitude towards the other children and not be so bossy, and that in their weekly reports they will stress the favourable results rather than the unfavourable ones. We persuade them to make their report in the form of a little composition.

The following are some of the weekly reports made by various leaders:

1. TEN TO TWELVE-YEAR-OLD BOYS

Group Report No. 3. No. 24 is, as always, a reliable comrade. He is excellent in mathematics. No. 2 could co-operate a bit more than he does. He knows quite a lot but can't bring himself to say it. Otherwise there isn't much to complain of. No. 8 is also all right. No. 5 is a good fellow but he could co-operate more than he does, too. No. 32 is much better lately. In natural history and geometry he co-operates well.'

Group Report No. 4. No. 17 wouldn't get down from the platform when I asked him to. No. 19 did everything I asked him. No. 22 was all right, too. No. 23 sometimes wrestled with No. 8. No. 13 was all right. No. 29 often plays the fool.'

It is easy to see that these Group Leaders do not yet know what to put in their reports.

2. THIRTEEN TO FOURTEEN-YEAR-OLD BOYS

Group Report No. 1. 'No. 31 has improved. But sometimes he's rowdy and then, as he puts it, "Someone's for it!" Something happened yesterday I didn't like. I don't think it's decent when a boy denounces his friend over a broken glass pipe. I won't mention the name of the boy, but I don't believe No. 31 deliberately broke his pipe. No. 18 is doing very well. On Tuesday he sat quietly in his place and read for a long time and then turned to look at what the others were doing. On Wednesday it was the same. No. 7 is getting on much better. On Thursday he brought his home-made Punch and Judy Show to school. Of course, there was a sensation, and we didn't find it easy to keep the boys quiet. No. 7 is all right except that he does tear around a good bit. But on Thursday he was all right, just walked up and down.'

Group Report No. 2. 'No. 15 has made great strides in foreign languages; he's one of the best now. No. 15 worked hard. If anyone made mistakes on the blackboard he corrected them. Our teacher gave him a particularly difficult sentence to write and he did it without a mistake. In mathematics he also works hard. In the percentage calculation each of us had to report his result separately, and all his fourteen sums were right. No. 4 used to tell tales a lot, but he's got much better lately. He's no longer quite so talkative and boastful. But on Friday he disturbed our foreign language lesson a good deal. His paintbox fell down, and some of the china dishes got broken. An ink-pot also fell down. It didn't break but the ink was spilt over the floor. And now about his quarrel with No. 23. No. 23 said to me: "Look, No. 4 has upset the ink and he doesn't want to wipe it up." The squabble went on, but in the end No. 4 had to wipe up the ink. In this way, of course, we lost a good deal of time. Perhaps it would be a good idea if the two were separated.'

As the reports show, the leaders do not concern themselves only with the behaviour of the other boys but also with their school work.

The development of a leader from a sort of policeman into a helper is, it must be admitted, the most difficult part of the whole problem of school self-government. The following are amongst the chief difficulties:

1. *Arrogance* on the part of the leaders and a desire to satisfy their urge to self-assertion. Again and again it is obvious that in the beginning the post of a 'leader' is very much desired, because, in particular, many children regard it as an opportunity for ordering others around. They mistake the appearance, which flatters their vanity, for the reality. We have to reckon with this sort of egoism. There is no point in adopting an ostrich-like policy and perhaps abandoning the self-government experiment merely in order to side-step the opportunity for egoism. Would the latent egoism be non-existent just because it had less opportunity to express itself? It is better that the egoism should be allowed to come to the surface, where the teacher can deal with it appropriately. The following illuminating incident goes to confirm this view:

In one of our classes we had a ten-year-old boy who was polite, tidy and a good worker. For weeks he was regarded as an exemplary pupil. But on one occasion during the weekly discussion he came out with the following proposal: the teacher should secretly give one or two of the boys instruction to provoke other children to mischief during the break; the evil-doers should then be severely punished. None of us would have dreamt that this particular boy was capable of making such a proposal. And what was still more surprising, several of the other youngsters enthusiastically supported his proposal. The incident lit up the real situation like a flash of lightning and showed the teacher that he had a good deal of educational spadework in front of him.

Where the urge for self-assertion is excessively strong the whole gamut of Individual-Psychological methods must be mobilized. The easiest thing of course, would be merely to dismiss such unsuitable leaders. However, our task is to divert the urge for self-assertion from a negative channel into a positive one. In many cases it will prove better to leave such leaders in their positions of responsibility whilst, at the same time, seeking to alter their life style by the methods of Individual Psychology. Examples of how this can be done will be given later.

2. *Subjectiveness, Favouritism.* This, too, can be changed only by thoroughly influencing the child in question.

3. *Tactlessness.* This failing is understandable when we realize that some of these boys are just left to the streets and have no opportunity of obtaining any polish, whilst others have been encouraged in a coarse and brutal life style.

4. *Lack of understanding* for the essential tasks of the leader. This arises from the mistaken belief that the leader can make an impression only by vehemence and intimidation.

5. *Lack of interest.* This comes from a lack of community feeling in general, or from the discouragement which sets in when a boy finds the tasks of his office more difficult than he expected.

6. *Failure to set an example.* A failure on the part of the leader to respect the laws of the community.

7. *Harsh criticism from classmates*, who see the failings and errors of the leader greatly magnified, whilst at the same time quite over-looking their own.

Obviously not all the boys who are appointed leaders will succeed in obtaining respect for the established standards of behaviour in a tactful and comradely fashion. After all, many adults would find it difficult to measure up to such standards.

On one occasion the children proposed as a composition theme: 'Criticism of our class community and proposals for its improvement.' The relationship between the class leaders and the class came in for a great deal of discussion. We produce particularly illuminating passages from a number of these compositions:

A leader: 'When the break comes and I see that one of the boys in my class is dashing around I take a comic, a book of riddles or something else that interests him and get him settled quietly down at his desk. But many Group Leaders don't care about the behaviour of their groups and they join in the rowdiness themselves.'

Pupil K: 'The Group Leaders are behaving like babies. They ought to take a firmer hold on things.'

Pupil W: 'The blackboard monitor does his job well but as soon as he's cleaned the blackboard it seems to provoke some of the boys and they go up and smear it over again. No wonder S. is getting fed up and talking about resigning.'

Pupil G: 'The nine o'clock break begins. Now it's like a sea. At first the waves just lap the shore, but after a minute or two a storm breaks out and then the waves smash down on the shore in tremendous breakers. There is chaos in the class. The Group Leaders tell the boys to go to their places. Self-control doesn't work at all.'

93

Monitors, Leaders and Helpers

Very often it is not long before a boy with a real talent for leadership is discovered. Intelligence, tact, zeal and a conciliatory attitude soon secure a considerable and obvious influence for him and win the appreciation of other children. One youngster writes: 'The boys follow him (the leader) because he understands how to deal with a class community. How would it be if every month we elected a new class leader? There would be no favouritism then. If one boy treated the other badly, then when the other boy was elected class leader he could have his revenge.' Thus, even a child who has obviously not yet found his proper place in the class community is unable to prevent himself expressing appreciation of the class leader.

The peak point of a leader's performance is reached when his own conduct is exemplary, when he succeeds in maintaining discipline, and when, to crown it all, he is able to open the discussion and to lead it when lessons begin. As an experiment we have often deliberately arrived late and found the work proceeding well under the leadership of one of the boys, and all the children busy.

If a leader turns out a failure, then we can adopt, in the appropriate form, all the methods and little tricks we discussed above. The method of guidance will often be used, generally in a talk between the teacher and the leader in question or at a meeting of leaders. The latter way has the advantage that all the leaders present can be similarly influenced, and this contributes considerably to securing uniformity in their methods.

Apart from monitors and class leaders, another type of function has grown out of the needs of our class work, that of the 'helper'. Let us illustrate how the function of helper comes into existence. In the German lesson a comparative test was made. After dictation the teacher corrected the work and noted the number of errors in orthography in each case. The result was then represented in the form of a graph on the blackboard. The graph showed clearly that some of the children were far below the reasonable demands which could be made of the particular age group (eleven to twelve years). The children were obviously impressed by the revelation.

Teacher No. 1: 'Well, what do you think of it?'

Pupil X: 'We'll have to do something about it. It won't do for four boys to lag behind the rest like that.'

A lively discussion then followed as to how matters could be improved and it was decided to organize help for those who failed to make the grade in German or mathematics or any of the chief subjects. In this way the institution of assistance in German and mathematics arose.

Each pupil who needed it was given a 'helper' to assist him. During the lesson this helper sat next to the boy in need of help. That meant some temporary reorganization of the seating arrangements, but the problem was soon settled. The helper had to keep a watchful eye on his protégé, and any disturbance of the class in consequence of these partnerships was raised in class or individual discussions and remedied.

Some of the helpers got together with their protégés outside school hours. They voluntarily sacrificed their free time to do the job they had undertaken. Of course, needless to say, sometimes where the spirit was willing the flesh proved weak.

This helper system was, as an opportunity for training, a very welcome supplement to our efforts to encourage the more backward children to improve. Later on the boys organized their own supplementary lessons. Without any pressure the helpers and their protégés would get together for a couple of hours every Monday afternoon for 'German' and in the same way every Friday afternoon for 'Mathematics'. And finally one or two of the boys with good handwriting organized a 'handwriting course'. It was supervised by a teacher, who, however, took no direct part in the work, and the lessons, the setting of tasks, dictation and the correction of mistakes, etc., were all carried out by the helpers. The teachers seldom intervened and they contented themselves with giving general hints. Otherwise, the boys did their own work. The organizing ability displayed by the helpers was often astonishing. The work was always adapted to the needs of those to be helped.

On such afternoons the classroom was a lively place. At one desk a pair would be sitting: one dictating zealously from a book provided by the teacher, and the other writing it all down. at first rather unwillingly and perhaps even a little resentfully, but gradually with increasing interest until finally he was working enthusiastically. In one corner a helper would sit firing the multiplication table at his protégé. Faster and faster would come the questions: 'Six times four?' 'Seven times eight?' And so on. Sometimes the protégé would hesitate; at other times the answer would come pat. In another corner a helper would get his protégé to read aloud and then carefully correct every wrong emphasis and mistake and read it out perfectly himself. Elsewhere a helper would assist a new boy to master the normal way of writing in the class. And so on.

95

Some of the protégés were given 'permanent subscriptions' for assistance, as one boy put it. Others would be released from the further necessity of taking supplementary lessons—a solemn moment this. Some of the protégés were even promoted to be helpers themselves.

This helper system developed and extended by its own inner logic. Absent pupils were given their tasks. Where a boy was unable to attend school for a while his helper would even go to his home. The helper system extended beyond the purely educational sphere, and the boys decided to provide a 'knocker-up' who undertook to call on the boy at his home in good time and to bring him along to school. This measure rapidly obviated the symptom of evasion and truant-playing. One boy who was particularly grubby in his work was promised the appointment of a special 'cleaner', and this, together with the influence of the teacher, soon mended matters. The boys even began to help each other socially; they shared their sandwiches, invited other boys home to lunch, prepared little presents for them, and so on. One day a group of boys came to the teacher with a small sum of money and the request: 'Please give this to N. so that he can get his hair cut and look neater and cleaner.' The eyes of children don't miss much!

Thus the class as a community of assistance represents the crown of the whole system. The most important achievement of the whole system of school self-government seems to us to lie in the fact that it encourages children to realize the difficulties of others and to come forward and help instead of standing coldly and disinterestedly to one side. But it is not always the thing itself that matters. Even a social attitude can have an egoistic motive flattering to the individual adopting it. Our real aim must be 'Social Behaviour for Social Reasons'. That is the point.

CHAPTER VII

The Weekly Discussion Hour

The author once had an illuminating object lesson when visiting a children's home in Germany. When he asked what happened when children proved unable to find their place in the community he was told: 'Every month there is a general meeting of children and teachers and a vote is taken on the conduct of each child. Whoever does not succeed in gaining at least four votes in his favour is expelled from the home.'

This idea of the community as something which is entitled to table uncompromising demands to which the individual has to conform under pain of expulsion is totally inadequate in the light of Individual Psychology. The aim of Individual Psychology is not merely to educate the child in fulfilling the demands which the community makes upon him. What is presupposed in our class discussions is an understanding approach to the errors of its individual members, a desire to help these members of the community by revealing to them the secret aims behind their actions, and, by offering them encouragement and the possibility of success experiences, to assist them forward in the future.

From the point of view of educating the child for the community, such intimate discussion hours are indispensable. Proceeding from the specific case we move forward to an understanding of the underlying motives, revealing what was not consciously realized, and thus encouraging self-realization—the necessary condition for all self-education. The following records of discussions must be regarded only as the first steps in a practice which is founded on this theoretical recognition that education through the community is possible only if the community supplements its proper demands on the individual by

G
97

an understanding of his errors and a revelation of their real motives, and by assisting the individual in an individual fashion.

EXAMPLE OF A CLASS DISCUSSION (AGES 11 TO 12)

The Group Leader makes his report:

'S. is beginning to grow up. He co-operates with the others now, but he still doesn't seem to have any friends. B. often doesn't reply when he's spoken to. I. is improving, but there's still a long way to go. B. seems to be afraid to open his mouth. I think he hesitates to do anything for fear someone else will do better. And then there are half a dozen boys who just won't let anyone else get a word in edgeways. C. is lazy. . . .'

Pupil G: 'I'm new here, but I think the Group Leader oughtn't to show up the other boys like that. He ought to talk only about the class as a whole, not about individual boys. It isn't his business to make reproaches. It's the teacher's job to say So-and-so has improved, and So-and-so has done something wrong; not the Group Leader's.'

Teacher No. 1: 'G. hasn't been with us long enough to realize what we are really after. It ought to be explained to him.'

Pupil B: 'After all, we have decided that the Group Leader should make reports.'

Pupil F: 'When we first came to school we were all pretty rotten fellows. We've been going to school now for four years and we're not much better. But in the upper school we are educated differently. We have agreed that boys should be elected as Class Leaders or Group Leaders. The three Group Leaders should be in command during the breaks, and the Class Leader should be in command of the whole class.'

Teacher No. 1: 'Some of you are smiling. One of you seems to be annoyed. I wonder what it is he doesn't like.'

Pupil H: 'The words "rotten fellows".'

Pupil F: 'No, it's the word "command".'

Pupil B: 'When a master isn't present the Class Leader has to take his place. The Group Leaders have to report on what goes on in the break, for instance, when a boy gets into a fight.'

Pupil G: 'That's all no answer to what I said.'

Teacher No. 1: 'It's not clear enough to G. yet.'

Pupil G: 'What I mean is the Group Leader mentions names. He shouldn't do that. He oughtn't to say: "So-and-so's improving. So-

and-so did this, that or the other." No one ought to talk about his classmates like that.'

Pupil H (vastly astonished): 'But that's what the class discussion is for, so that we can talk about everything.'

Pupil R: 'G. means that the Group Leader tells tales. But that's a mistake. We are out to help. When the Group Leader says: "So-and-so has gone backwards in mathematics," that's not tale-telling. It's for us to help if that's the case. That's what the extra lessons are for. And the discussion hour is for us to learn how, for instance, K. is getting on.'

Pupil B: 'I don't know how it is with the others, but when I hear in the weekly discussion that I've done well, I feel pleased.'

Teacher No. 1: 'I think everyone feels the same. Of course, there are always some who pretend they aren't interested. They just like to think they're above it all. I think G. will now begin to understand what it is we're after. We don't do all this to make one boy feel pleased and the other boy feel small. As R. pointed out, we want to help. The Group Leader mentioned S. Now S. gave us a lot of trouble at one time, for six whole months. Sometimes it was a great nuisance. And then things suddenly began to improve. Teacher No. 2 has even told me that they're going very well now. I could hardly believe my ears. What's the result?'

Several boys: 'He is no longer so babyish. He joins in the work. He doesn't play any more tricks.'

Teacher No. 1: 'He did well at grammar today.' (Turning to Pupil S.) 'Now you can stick out your chest—or try to do even better. Whichever you think is best.'

Pupil F: 'S. wouldn't be any trouble at all now if B. would sometimes show him things.'

Pupil B: 'I do show him when necessary, but he's always coming to me and he only does it to disturb me.'

Pupil T: 'We ought to put someone of the same sort next to him so that he can see what it's like.'

Teacher No. 1: 'I think he'd stop it then!'

Pupil B (to the teacher): 'Do you mind if S. sits somewhere else? Let him change places.'

Pupil P: 'S. ought to be put next to a good pupil.'

Teacher No. 1: 'We have already discussed the point and agreed that the helper should always sit next to the boy to be helped. The only question is, does it work?'

Pupil H: 'After sums they can change places again.'

Pupil R: 'Someone who can't do his lessons very well ought always to have someone who can sit next to him. Teacher No. 2 drew up a table. Everyone ought to say whether he's in agreement with it or not.'

Teacher No. 1: 'Is there anything else urgent?'

Several boys: 'The library.'

Teacher No. 1: 'I think it's got a bit late for that today. Time flies. How many of you are still able to stand up to attention?' (The children stand up to take their leave.) 'After five hours of it we've had enough. I know that we can ask a lot of you, and you can all do it. But all I want you to do now is to leave quietly and in a disciplined fashion. Thank you.'

EXAMPLE OF A CLASS DISCUSSION (AGES 12 TO 13)

(Preliminary remarks: The boys keep notebooks in geography, physics and natural science. Special attention is paid to the teaching of economic geography, and graphs and economic statistics play a big role. Some of the boys keep their notebooks very carefully. This means hard work and takes up a good deal of time. However, at the beginning of the school year a new natural science master has arrived, who asks only for rapidly executed sketches. After a few weeks the contradiction in the demands makes itself felt and the boys begin to protest against the more exacting way of working still required of them in geography and physics. An impression of passive resistance is created. It showed itself particularly in the geography lesson. The problem is then raised in the next class discussion.)

Geography Teacher: 'Problems have arisen during the last few days with which we must deal now.'

Pupil A: 'Let the Class Leader start the discussion.'

Class Leader: 'Some of us have discussed amongst ourselves doing without the notebooks. It's something that interests us all.'

Geography Teacher: 'That means me, too!' (With good humour.) 'That's grand!'

Pupil B: 'Perhaps the teacher thinks we're organizing a conspiracy against him?'

Geography Teacher: 'No, I don't suppose the matter is as serious as all that. I'm sure that you don't intend to have me beheaded straight away.'

Pupil R: 'We want to discuss how we're going to work in the future; whether we keep on with the notebooks or whether we work in the way the natural science master wants.'

Pupil F: 'But teacher has told us that we must have the notebooks because otherwise we haven't any proper records.'

Pupil B: 'Nobody has anything against the notebooks, but teacher wants them kept carefully, and that takes up too much time. In that time we could be learning something else.'

Pupil R: 'And what about someone who does his best to keep his notebook neat and finds he can't succeed?'

Pupil H: 'Some teachers have been here for eighteen years. Every teacher has his own way of teaching and his own way of working. But some of the boys say: "The natural science master should do this or that." That's not right!'

Pupil P: 'B says the notebook is a waste of time. But we haven't any textbooks in geography and therefore we must have notebooks.'

Pupil H: 'That ought to settle it, I think.'

Pupil R: 'But we also have a notebook with the natural science master, though with him we make our entries at school, as we go along. Of course, it's not as neat as when we do it at home.'

Pupil F: 'The geography and physics teachers don't like loose notes. We should buy ourselves proper notebooks. They don't cost much.'

Geography Teacher: 'If I understand you boys rightly, you think it's an unnecessary burden that you should have to enter up all your notes once again at home, but more carefully. Perhaps you might think it over and ask yourself why that terrible man demands neat and careful notes. Ask yourself why he isn't satisfied with your just writing it down?'

Pupil H: 'It's not good for a boy to get used to scribbling. If he gets a job in an office when he leaves school he might get the sack for scribbling.'

Pupil R: 'I don't suppose there'd be time enough in business to jot things down first and then enter them up neatly afterwards. It would be better therefore if we got used to writing down everything neatly in the first place.'

Pupil F: 'That's all very well, but we've got to think of the future. We do everything neatly and accurately at school. But in business you've got to work quickly.'

Pupil K: 'We are arguing about whether we should keep a notebook or not. I think it's much better to keep a neat and orderly notebook because at the same time we learn to work independently and to repeat what we've learnt.'

Pupil F: 'Let's take a vote on it.'

Pupil Z: 'There's no sense in voting. It's already decided that we need notebooks because we haven't any textbooks.'

Pupil R: 'Let those who want to keep a notebook, keep one; the others needn't.'

Pupil L: 'But Z. has already said that we need a notebook because we haven't any textbooks. The notebook is our own home-made textbook. We can't look up things if we haven't got a notebook.'

Pupil R: 'We can look up scribbled notes just as well.'

Pupil G: 'But scribbled notes are generally flung away at the end of the year.'

Teacher No. 2: 'How many of you still have your loose notes from last year?' (Nine of the boys put up their hands.) 'And how many of you still have your notebooks?' (Twenty-nine of the boys put up their hands.)

Pupil N: 'You can see from that!'

Pupil E: 'There you are!' (General movement in the class.)

Pupil K: 'I propose that whoever wants to keep a notebook should do so, but no one should be judged on whether he keeps a notebook or not, but only on what he can do.'

Pupil M: 'Let's agree to that, and at the end of six months we can compare the boys who keep notebooks with those who don't and see who's best.'

Pupil H: 'That's a wrong way of looking at it. In geography, and in history too, the main thing is that we learn something. What a boy can do is the chief thing. But where the notebook is concerned it's the form that matters.'

Pupil R: 'You can't make up your mind. In the break you got quite excited and talked very differently.'

Geography Teacher: 'There's no harm in that. I think it's a good thing when a boy learns something from the discussion and changes his mind when he sees good reason to change it. After all, that's just why we do discuss things.'

Pupil K: 'In my opinion we ought to go on keeping notebooks, but the way in which they're kept shouldn't count in geography.'

Pupil R: 'In geometry a proper notebook isn't necessary; just a notebook is enough.'

The Weekly Discussion Hour

Geography Teacher: 'It seems as though some of the boys don't like the notebook. I wonder why that is.'

Pupil K (mockingly): 'In the time it takes to enter up the notebook properly they could be playing football.'

Pupil S: 'You needn't try to be funny, K. Some of the boys think they can't write so well. The teacher can always tell whether a boy is trying or not.'

Pupil R: 'I often make up my mind to write nicely. For a while it goes quite well, but then suddenly I can't do it any more. I want to write nicely always, but I can't no matter how hard I try.'

Geography Teacher: 'As long as a boy is really trying he won't come to much harm. But with that I think we've come to a very important point. One of you said that the teacher knows how much he can ask of a boy. The teacher knows, he said, that not all boys can work equally well. R. said that he found such work very difficult; no matter how hard he tries, his work will never be as good as, for instance, that of L.'

Pupil R: 'I just can't do it. I'm just not so good at it.'

Teacher No. 1: 'I think that R. has just expressed the real trouble very clearly. I know from my own experience how the thing happens. When I went to school there was one of the boys whose homework was always wonderfully neat. We used to admire it and wonder how he did it, and then one day we discovered the secret. He used to write it out several times before he was satisfied with it. In other words, he just practised more than we did. Why do I tell you that? Because I want you to see that it's not true to say: some boys can and other boys just can't. If one boy is better at a thing than another, it is because he has practised it more. Let us take one boy who does something very well. Another boy now practises so long that he can do it too. But we mustn't forget that in the meantime the first boy has been practising still further and can do it better than ever. Thus it isn't easy to catch up with another boy. But because it isn't easy to catch up with another boy, we mustn't assume that it's a waste of time to try. If you do try you will make progress. Think of how much you have all learnt since you first came to school! Clever boys will perhaps now understand why R. is so much opposed to the notebook. Perhaps he will already have realized why himself. I don't think there can be much dispute about it now. Whoever does his work neatly has killed several birds with one stone: first of all, as he writes he learns: secondly, he recapitulates everything we have discussed, and thus makes it easier for himself to learn, and, thirdly, he is improving his handwriting. Whoever thinks it better that way, above all, whoever isn't afraid of difficulties, I will ask to keep a notebook. But at the same time I agree with some of the boys who said that what you know is the chief thing, and therefore we shall count the notebook only for industry and form marks.'

Pupil: 'That settles the matter then.'

EXAMPLE OF A CLASS DISCUSSION (AGES 12 TO 13)

(Six children, about the most intelligent boys in the class, have formed a secret association. The class as a whole heard about the existence of the association only when one of the members was expelled and then gave the game away. The revelation that a few of the boys had separated themselves from the rest caused great indignation in the class. Most of the children regarded it as a breach of class solidarity.)

1st Member of the Association: 'Well, we really wanted to keep it dark, but seeing that it has come out now in class, we shall have to talk about it. The fact is that we were saving up on our own so that No. 5 could go on our class outing with us.'

Pupil 1: 'I don't think secret associations ought to be formed. Some boys might want to join and then not be accepted. But it's no use forbidding it. If it were forbidden then they would go on doing it in secret.'

1st Member of the Association: 'Of course! We should do it outside the school where it isn't forbidden.'

Pupil 2: 'But when you behave mysteriously and use a secret code amongst yourselves, how much is left of the class community?'

2nd Member of the Association (rather excitedly): 'Well, tell us what we've done wrong then.'

Interruption: 'Don't get so excited!'

Pupil 2: 'It's you who've made all the fuss and mystery about it. Not us.'

Great excitement. The children all talk at once. They get more and more excited. In the meantime the teacher is calmly writing on the blackboard:

The Weekly Discussion Hour

Class Community	Association
?	Secrecy

Object:

To help	To help
Positive	Negative

Teacher No. 2: 'And now, thank goodness, the class has reached boiling-point. Perhaps you can now all calm down a bit.' (Pause.) 'Once, when I was a boy, I was a member of such a secret association. Although in those days, of course, we hadn't such a thing as a "class community". That certainly makes a big difference. Perhaps those boys who haven't taken any part in the discussion yet can tell us what they think of it. As far as I can see, it's very much as usual; there is some good in it, but also some danger.'

3rd Member of the Association: 'Tell us, first of all, what there is wrong about it.'

Pupil 3: 'That the whole thing was kept secret.'

Teacher No. 2: 'The facts are now out. The tension is visible. Let the class express its opinions.'

1st Member of the Association: 'If thirty-six children save up the result is better than when only six do.'

Teacher No. 2 (writes up on the blackboard): 'Thirty-six is better than six.'

Teacher No. 2: 'That is a mathematical truth.'

Pupil 4 (suddenly): 'Why was one of the boys expelled from the association?'

Teacher No. 2: 'That's all part of it. It's dramatic. People often die in dramas.' (General laughter. The excitement has died down.)

2nd Member of the Association: 'Before Christmas we agreed that we should all save up for the outing. The whole class. Well, have you all saved up?'

Teacher No. 2: 'Now let the other boys tell us what they think about it. Their views are very important.' (He writes on the blackboard: "Subjective views—Objective views".) 'The physicists are always arguing amongst themselves. That's the reason why they have made so much progress.'

Pupil 5: 'No. Quite the opposite. They always work together.'

Pupil 6: 'But there's a big difference between a friend and an association.'

The Weekly Discussion Hour

(Pause. The children study the last words written up on the blackboard.)

Teacher No. 1: 'And now the discussion has suddenly come to a stop. Yes, it's difficult to avoid the personal pronoun!'

2nd Member of the Association (turning to Pupil 6): 'Did the association do any harm to the class? Did we deprive you of anything?'

(The excitement rises again.)

Teacher No. 2: 'Let those speak who are not boiling inwardly with indignation and turning round and round like a dog chasing its own tail.'

Pupil 4: 'You want to feel yourselves big and therefore you form an association. You harm the class's good name.'

1st Member of the Association: 'If we wanted to make ourselves big would we have said anything about it?'

Pupil 6: 'You didn't say anything! It's we who found out about it.'

1st Member of the Association: 'You don't save up at all. And it doesn't do at all that you should bring a few pennies while another boy brings ten shillings.'

Pupil 7: 'You're talking personally again and not objectively.'

1st Member of the Association: 'We are saving for D. and not for ourselves.'

Pupil 6: 'And you don't go to the cinema?'

2nd Member of the Association: 'Yes, when we've got too much money (general laughter) we go with our friends to the cinema.'

Pupil 8: 'Everything's getting all mixed now. One minute he's talking about friendship and the next minute about the association.'

1st Member of the Association: 'Everything has been said now. It's time the class decided whether it's going to tolerate the association or not. If it won't, then we'll continue it outside the school.'

Interruption: 'Why not let the whole class join in?'

2nd Member of the Association: 'It's nobody's business what happens outside the school.'

Teacher No. 1 to Teacher No. 2: 'We have ringside seats at a first-class community battle.'

Pupil 1: 'Why don't you want us all to save?'

Teacher No. 1: 'The association says that its object was to help D. But I can imagine the best way to help D.'

1st Member of the Association: 'But we need money in order to help. That's why the association saved up.'

Teacher No. 1: 'If you really want to help then you must go a bit further. What do you think?'

Pupil 6: 'Many must take part.'

1st Member of the Association: 'That's not true. Let's make the experiment. Let the whole class save up and at the end of three weeks we'll see who's saved up most, the whole class or us six.'

(Teacher No. 2 writes on the blackboard: 'Association savings plus class savings—D.') (The name of the boy in question.)

Teacher No. 2 (very thoughtfully): 'D. stands there with both hands held out; one to the right and the other to the left. In the one he gets the money of the association and in the other he gets the money of the class.'

Pupil 7: 'That's not fair, that he should get both!'

Teacher No. 1: 'If we did it like that then no doubt a good deal of money would be collected. D. would do very well out of it. But perhaps others would suffer? Why do boys save up, anyhow? I think the time has come to look behind the scenes as we have done so often already. Saving up is the stage setting. Is there any boy in this class who can see behind the setting?'

Pupil 5: 'Behind the setting a big battle is going on.'

Pupil 9: 'Behind the setting is ambition.'

Teacher No. 1: 'Still more than that.'

Pupil 2: 'Vanity.'

Pupil 6: 'Pleasures, too: the cinema.'

Pupil 4: 'Let the class decide whether the association is to continue to exist or not. Or whether the whole class is to save up.'

Pupil 1: 'Let's have a school outings' fund to which all contribute.'

Teacher No. 2: 'It's not much use coming to any decision now because everyone is too excited. The decision wouldn't be carried out.'

Pupil 3: 'Let's vote all the same.'

1st Member of the Association: 'We won't save any more in school and we won't set ourselves up against the class. Our association resigns.'

(General astonishment and a long silence.)

Teacher No. 2: 'The proposal or the declaration apparently doesn't satisfy everybody.'

Pupil 3: 'It isn't in the spirit of our community.'

Pupil 2: 'They'll only go on saving in secret.'

Teacher No. 2: 'Try out what they suggest. . . .'

Pupil 8: 'They'll only go on doing it outside.'

Pupil 4: 'Then we'll have the whole trouble all over again.'

1st Member of the Association: 'If you aren't in agreement then we'll go into another class, that's all.'

Several boys: 'Go then.'

1st Member of the Association (jumping up excitedly): 'That's a problem. Is the class community to be carried on only in the class or outside as well?'

Pupil 3: 'What does it matter to us what a few boys do in the street?'

Teacher No. 1: 'That really is a problem. There's something in it. Which of you boys will succeed in finding it out? Think it over until our next discussion.'

Continuation of the discussion a week later. The boys are still very excited.

Pupil 3: 'In the gym lesson two members of the association said. . . .'

2nd Member of the Association: 'We haven't got any association.'

(Laughter. General disturbance.)

Teacher No. 2: 'We're about to turn this into an entertainment. I'm in favour of discussing the matter seriously or not at all.'

Pupil 3: 'But W., you told me straight that you had an association. You've already admitted it.'

1st Member of the Association: 'We got on together so well at the outing that we decided to stay together and often have outings.'

Pupil 4: 'But have you got an association or not?'

1st Member of the Association: 'The class can't stop us from forming a group!'

2nd Member of the Association: 'We want to go together on all outings because we got on so well together at the last one.'

Pupil 3: 'But you keep yourselves away from the rest of us in class too. One of you said to me, "You don't belong to us." '

(General excitement in the class.)

Teacher No. 1: 'Is every boy accepted into this association?'

Pupil 2 (jumping up): 'No, that's not so. They wouldn't take F.'

3rd Member of the Association: 'You've got to prove that we've broken the law of the class community.'

Pupil 3: 'You expel boys in the break. That's a known fact. What sort of a class community is that?'

4th Member of the Association: 'We had to send a few of the boys

108

away because they wanted to split on us, and F. started kicking.'

Pupil F: 'All right, I admit that. I did kick. But I was angry because you were always saying, "Go away!"' '

Teacher No. 2: 'So the business went from bad to worse. Like this discussion. I should like to propose. . . .'

Pupil 9: 'Let the class decide whether the association may exist in the school or only outside.'

Teacher No. 2 (writes up on the blackboard): 'Class Community—Group' and then observes calmly: 'Some people think there's an insoluble contradiction there. Other people think that both can exist quite satisfactorily side by side. Some of you are finding it difficult to think straight because personal rancour is involved; the others are finding it difficult because they are being asked to give up something they like. Some of you feel that you have been humiliated. Many of you think the class itself is small enough and that still smaller groups aren't necessary. A great deal of passion is finding an outlet in the discussion.'

Pupil 9: 'There always will be rancour because the other boys want to hear what you whisper to each other in corners. You make them wild.'

Teacher No. 2: 'But we have always had separate groups in the class: for shorthand, violin playing, for extra lessons, and so on. And no one has ever objected. So I think there must be something about this particular group which is different.'

1st Member of the Association: 'I don't know whether I ought to say it but I think the others are a bit jealous of us. First of all because one of us has really done something, which is unusual: he rose from the second-class group into the first. And secondly, we have boys amongst us with splendid marks.'

Teacher No. 2 (draws a wall on the blackboard): 'Now that was the class at one time. A solid wall. Now there's a breach in it, and the breach is getting larger and larger. (Draws the breach in the wall.) Now is that a satisfactory state of affairs? For my part, I doubt it.'

Pupil 9: 'It's the secrecy that does it. The boys don't like it. You never know what's going on. It makes everything uncertain.'

Teacher No. 2 (goes on writing calmly on the blackboard): 'Secrecy—uncertainty.' 'Now the point is not whether that's true or not, but whether the other boys think it is; whether they feel uncertain. We learnt something about that during the war.' (All the boys are listening very attentively.) 'In the night, behind every stone and bush, there seemed to be steps and whisperings. Yet there was really nothing at all. It was a shabby sort of feeling! Such a state of war exists in the class now. If we were to forbid the group it would go on existing under the surface. It's a difficult business.'

2nd Member of the Association: 'It's we who feel insecure. We can be betrayed. They have planned to interfere with us, to listen to everything we say and then split on us.'

Teacher No. 1 turns to Teacher No. 2: 'When I was a little boy I used to play a very amusing game. Some children still play it. You need a small basin, some soapy water and a straw. And then you can blow wonderful iridescent bubbles. They looked beautiful, but when you tried to catch one it burst and there was nothing left.'

4th Member of the Association: 'Teacher is attacking us now. Castles in the air. But we'll prove we aren't building any castles in the air.'

Teacher No. 2: 'We must think still more over what's happened. A group has formed itself. Other boys are standing outside. Is that right, or isn't it? Try to think straight without passion. Is that right from the standpoint of good comradeship? Is it, or isn't it? Even if you have to give up something you prize. . . . It's quite an intelligence test. It would be a good thing if each boy thought it out for himself. . . . Don't let yourself get excited about it. . . . Such things are constantly cropping up in life. Now we'll see how serious the class community is.'

Continuation of the discussion a week later. The boys are still excited.

1st Member of the Association: 'We have worked out conditions which everyone who is a member of the association must comply with. Let the teacher read them out and then everyone will know what he's got to do if he wants to become a member of our association.'

Teacher No. 2: 'You can do that very well yourself.'

1st Member of the Association: 'Our conditions are: 1. No unpunctuality. 2. Bring tasks along. 3. Maintain discipline. 4. Bring along at least one brick.'

Pupil No. 2: 'I'd like to know whether those conditions have got to be fulfilled before joining or after.'

1st Member of the Association: 'Before joining, but we allow a trial period.'

Pupil 7: 'Then you're not an improvement association. Some of us would be excluded.'

1st Member of the Association: 'In time the boys would learn.'

Pupil No. 8: 'Oh, is that so? I think you're dreaming.'

2nd Member of the Association: 'No one can deny that G. has improved since he has been a member of our association. G. won't feel insulted when I point that out.'

Teacher No. 2: 'How is it? Some of the boys have to go through a trial period and others aren't invited to join at all. I imagine that quite a lot of boys would pass through the trial period satisfactorily.'

2nd Member of the Association: 'We did invite one boy to join. But the others only mocked us.'

Pupil 2: 'They invited No. 25. And like that they weaken our defence.'

2nd Member of the Association: 'What have you got to defend?'

Pupil 2: 'You started the battle. On the streets you shouted, "We won! You were defeated!"'

Pupil 3: 'You shouted, "The teachers are on our side!"'

Pupil 4: 'Now everybody is getting angry again.'

Pupil 10 (innocent, peaceable and naïvely honest): 'I should like to suggest to the association that it accepts all the boys as members, and then keeps those who comply with the conditions.'

(General astonishment.)

Teacher No. 2: 'Is that a proposal? Shall we vote on it?'

3rd Member of the Association: 'I am against voting on it. We members of the association would be outvoted.' (Very excited.) 'We are in a minority.'

Teacher No. 2 (addressing Pupil 10): 'We understand you very well. But you're on ahead.' (To the whole class.) 'I'll make a proposal. I invite you all to think hard over the matter until the next discussion and try to discover what was wrong in your thinking about the whole affair. It will be a bright lad who finds out.'

Pupil 3: 'They won't say anything against themselves.'

Teacher No. 2: 'Oh, yes, they will. Amongst the members of the association there are certainly one or two who will admit it if they find where their thinking went wrong—even at the risk of hearing the others shout: "We've won!" I recognize the bona fides of all the members of the association.' (The expression is known to the children from previous discussions.) 'But there *is* an error in their thinking, though there's nothing dishonourable about that. Even the famous

111

mathematician Gauss made mistakes. That's not the important thing. So think it over and try to find out what the mistake was.'

Continuation of the discussion a week later. (We now present only the decisive concluding part of the discussion.)

Pupil 2: 'I asked what would happen if a boy who isn't good at his work wanted to join the association and one of them said: "He'd be thrown out." '

4th Member of the Association: 'You must have misunderstood.'

Pupil 8: 'There will be boys who don't want to belong to the association.'

2nd Member of the Association: 'That's just a disgrace to the boy if he doesn't want to be a good pupil.'

Pupil 10: 'K. said to me that I had done a lot of harm when I suggested that all the boys ought to be accepted into the group if they stand the trial successfully.'

Pupil K: 'I'm sorry, but I was wrong.'

Pupil 2: 'And I told them that it was all only boastfulness, and then K. said to me: "But you don't know our secrets." Well, isn't it it all just bragging and boasting and trying to be big?'

Teacher No. 1 to Teacher No. 2: 'Can't you imagine how someone must feel when he thinks the others admire him and suddenly someone says to him: "It's just all boasting!" '

Teacher No. 2: 'In the discussion when we first talked about the association things got very stormy. It's not so bad now. But the query about the mistake in thinking is still on the blackboard unsolved.'

Pupil 7: 'The boys have already given their opinion. Perhaps Teacher No. 2 can tell us his opinion now.'

Teacher No. 2: 'No, you can find out the mistake for yourselves.'

Pupil 2: 'The group attacked the community too much.'

Pupil 5: 'They were thinking too much of themselves.'

Pupil 8: 'They only thought of themselves and not about the possibility that others might feel hurt.'

Teacher No. 2: 'Couldn't help feeling hurt.'

1st Member of the Association: 'We didn't treat the others with sufficient consideration.'

Pupil 3: 'You drove a breach in the wall.'

Teacher No. 1: 'What do you call it when you sort things out in this fashion?'

Teacher No. 2: 'Think of the chemistry lessons you all like so much.'

Pupil 9: 'Analysis.'

Teacher No. 1 (writes on the blackboard):

> Association — Analysis
> Class Community — ?

Teacher No. 1: 'And what's the opposite?'

Pupil 9: 'Synthesis.'

Teacher No. 1: 'And what's the situation now?'

Pupil 9: 'Class community is synthesis, and the association is analysis.'

1st Member of the Association (jumping to his feet): 'We confused the two. That was where our thinking went wrong!'

(General commotion. He receives a few friendly pommels.)

Teacher No. 2: 'The mistake in thought was a confusion of two things. The members of the association thought they could build a community by splitting one.' (Very solemnly.) 'And now we ought to put up a memorial tablet. You're no longer excited about it all. The class community has arisen again.'

Pupil 3: 'A renaissance.' (The boys have learned about the Renaissance in their history lessons.)

Teacher No. 1 to Teacher No. 2: 'We'll enter it solemnly in our notebooks: "June 2nd 19. . . . The Day of Renaissance." '

CHAPTER VIII

The Problem Child

There is no doubt that in its manifold forms the community will favourably influence many of its members, but at the same time there will always be individuals who are so deeply discouraged that even this influence will prove insufficient to release them from their spiritual bonds. And it is here that the methods we have been describing find the limit of their effectiveness.

The further question arises: What is to be done with children who, despite the community of work, self-government, discussion and assistance, still do not change, still learn badly, still disturb the class, play the fool, act like gangsters, steal, lie, and so on?

A teacher must be far more than a mere leader. He must be a revealer and counsellor, a strategist, a trainer and a stage-manager. He must be able to develop all the dormant forces of the child. He must have a warm heart, but also a cool head to enable him to answer all the counter-moves of his charges on the chessboard of education. Whoever thinks that the school can educate by means of instruction alone, or within the framework of instruction, by granting the children self-government, is under-estimating the importance of the unknown forces operating in the soul of the child. The life style of a problem child can be changed only by individual treatment, and by this we do not mean merely that the teacher should take the peculiarities of the child into account, but that the individual treatment should be of a psychological nature.

The examples we are going to consider give a picture of these various functions of the teacher. The systematic order in which they are given should not, however, mislead the reader into supposing that things are always so greatly ordered in practice. Generally speaking, life does not lend itself to mechanical systematization. A teacher can rarely exercise his various functions in the tidy, chronological order given here; they will overlap, combine and replace each other, and only the sum total will give the final picture of reality.

The problem child—and the term goes farther than most people think—has taken a wrong road. But, for all that, there are still elements of community feeling in him. Although outwardly such a child may behave in a free and easy fashion as though he hadn't a care in the world, inwardly he is none too sure of himself. He is entangled in his error and there is nothing he fears more than the loss of his hard-won prestige in the eyes of the class and in the eyes of the teacher. Should he return, after all, to the useful side of life? For him that would represent defeat. The one thing such a child is anxious to avoid is to be made to look as though he has been defeated. Is that surprising? Are adults any different?

What! the child thinks to himself. I should give up my clowning? All my pals would lose interest in me if I did.

What! I should stop being lazy? If I did my father would immediately say: 'So I've driven it out of you at last!'

What! I should start being careful about my work? If I did the teacher would immediately say: 'So I've succeeded in knocking some sense into your head at last!'

What! I shouldn't get my own back when the chance comes? Why, I'd be ashamed of being so namby-pamby!

Need we go on? The return to the useful side of life is no easy matter for a lost sheep. If a boy tries then he is regarded with contempt by his former associates. They begun to laugh at him and tell him he's a coward.

'You haven't got any guts, that's why you are backing out.'

'You want to be one of teacher's goody-goodies.'

Anyone with a little experience of teaching knows how biting and wounding the words children use to each other can be.

The problem child has, therefore, the impression that if the struggle ends with his surrender to the community he has been, in some way, personally vanquished. He must necessarily regard the role of a repentant sinner as a humiliating one.

This is the point at which the teacher should intervene to relieve the child of his burden. He must smooth the child's path back.

'You seem to think that everyone is your enemy, and that you can keep your end up only if you are always fighting against everyone. You're always ready to spring at someone's throat. You seem to think that the world is a place in which a fellow is either on top as the victor or underneath as the defeated, brooding over revenges. And because that's the way you think it would look like a defeat if you changed your attitude. And you can't imagine anything worse than being defeated. But the fact is that the rest of us, your fellow pupils and I, are not out to defeat you at all. We don't even want to fight you. On the contrary, we want you to join us, work with us, go with us. If you do, I wouldn't dream of saying: "Ah! we've got William under, at last!" I can easily imagine a world in which there aren't only victors and vanquished. And I rather think you can, too—even if you won't admit it.'

The teacher must build bridges to make it easy for the child to beat a retreat without humiliation. He must show the child how he is misusing his physical powers as an excuse for going off in the wrong direction: show him, for example, how he is taking advantage of the fact, say, that he is left-handed in order to dodge the difficulties of learning to write properly; how he is misusing the abnormal formation of his vocal chords in order to dodge the difficulties of voice training; how he is misusing his poverty in a positive lust for all kinds of pleasure; how he is exploiting his pampering to pamper himself; how he is being tempted by his idea of growing up in a hostile environment to develop into an opposer on principle, and so on.

And in each case he must show the child just how he fell victim to his errors and let himself be drawn into this mistaken type of conduct. The deeper a child is involved and the more entangled he is psychologically, the more urgently the teacher must insist that, 'It's never too late to mend,' and give the child a liberating view of the life the community offers him.

Further, he must show the child the positive side of his negative conduct. The obstinate child must be shown his strength though the teacher must point out that he is using it for wrong ends. The child who is always playing the fool must be shown the magnitude of the efforts he makes, though the teacher must point out that he is using his powers wastefully. The insolent and daring boy must be shown his courage, though the teacher must point out that it is forcing him in the wrong direction. The grumbling, fault-finding child must be shown his sense of justice, which is apparently incorruptible, and so on. By identifying ourselves with the child in the first place, by apparently making ourselves his ally, we strengthen our contact with him on the one hand, and on the other, we relieve him of the feeling that: 'Well, that's how I am, even if I ought not to be.'

What we are after is to replace the fanatical belief of the child that he is what he is and that there is nothing to be done about it, with the belief in the possibility of a self-change. We must show him that because a thing is, it does not mean that it always must be. We must show him that mistakes do not mean that he must go on making mistakes, and that a boy can learn from his mistakes. There are a dozen and one ways of showing him this. And perhaps the best way of all is if the teacher uses himself as an object lesson, though a considerable degree of self-confidence is necessary for this. 'When I was your age....' Let no teacher fear that he will lose his authority if he tells the children anecdotes showing how he, too, made mistakes in his youth. In fact, the author can assure his readers that nothing is more conducive to the establishment of close and friendly contact than such a truly human approach to the children. And in any case, make no mistake, if a teacher pretends to have been a model child in his youth his charges will not believe him.

To give a child relief means to free him from the blockade of hopelessness, to clear the way for the self-development of the personality. The course of the ship of life is being directed by an invisible helmsman. He guides the ship as he has been instructed to do in childhood, at a time when the child who gave him his instructions had no idea of the rocks and reefs of life. Such an invisible helmsman knows his job only too well. He is a wizard. One child he saves from the troubles and trials of an examination and spares him all the searching questions of the examiners by giving him a splitting headache. Another child he provides with the necessary 'forgetfulness' so that the child has an excuse for not doing what he ought whilst at the same time retaining his prestige. Another child is provided with the lovely harbours of solitude so that he feels no desire to sail into the safe harbours of community life. . . .

The task is to show the child that this invisible helmsman who is guiding his life is none other than the child himself. If we want to bring about a self-realization we must discover what situations in earliest childhood first produced the fateful error which led to the self-induced veering of the ship off the proper course. The self-realization can be effected either by means of something or someone outside the child (lecture, drama, biography) or by direct approach to the child himself.

Here is an example of the first method:

Pupil S. was rather an ugly child. He was short-sighted and he even had a slight squint. He experienced great difficulties in mastering the problems raised by school and in particular the problem of establishing a proper relationship with the community. The revelation of his life style was brought about by indirect means.

A short story entitled 'Four Eyes', was read to the class. It was about a short-sighted boy who had to wear glasses and was laughed at and mocked by his playmates in consequence and who therefore began to live an anti-social life marked by hostility to the community. But then he made the acquaintance of a girl living in poor circumstances who gave him his first experience of a community attachment. To the extent that he now began to realize the error of his anti-social attitude, his share in the interests of the community increased. Finally he married the girl and became the mayor of the place in which he lived.

The story fitted S. like a glove. For him 'Four Eyes' was himself, and the revelation of the fundamental error: 'I am Four Eyes and therefore only a second-class person' which took place in the story helped S. to realize the error which was operating in himself. As in addition to this fundamental realization which came to S. the reading of the story also brought about a change in the attitude of his comrades towards him, the onerous inhibition was removed and S. developed into a good scholar and a good comrade.

The opportunity of revealing a way of life in this graphic fashion on the basis of an outside example will not often arise. In general, the teacher will have to use the second method.

The self-realization induced by a more direct approach to the child himself can relate to a single mistake. Pupil G. played truant from the shorthand lesson, which was held in the afternoon, on two successive occasions. Shorthand, it should be added, was not an obligatory subject. When he was asked the reason G. replied: 'I'd like to leave the class. I'm not interested in shorthand.'

As the 'flight from reality to the useless side of life' had already been fairly frequently discussed in the class, the teacher spoke to G. in the following fashion:

'Oh, so shorthand doesn't interest you? That's rather handy, isn't it? You can kill two birds with one stone. So you're not interested. But that's very much the same as saying: "I'm lazy," you know. Or: "It's my forgetfulness." We've often spoken about that sort of thing, haven't we? You'll remember how it works: the "forgetful" boy kills two birds with one stone. At the same time he has a good conscience about it. And you say: "I'm suffering from a lack of interest." How does that come about?'

G. lowers his head.

Teacher: 'The fact that you're not looking me in the face shows me that you know already.' (Pause.) 'You have already understood what's behind it when a boy says: "That doesn't interest me." ' (Pause.) 'Well, what about it? Will you go on with your shorthand or would you sooner have to say to yourself every time the shorthand lesson comes round: "Well, I'm well shot of that—but I'm a coward all the same." '

G: 'I'll go on with my shorthand.'

If the teacher is not out to reveal a single error but wishes to bring a child to a self-realization of a whole incorrect life style then he must help the child to realize what he has already realized, and he must do it in a way the child can understand. It is impossible to give any general recipe for this: everything depends on the particular circumstances of the case.

The sequence we propose here is intended only to give the reader an incidental idea of the direction in which the process must develop.

1. A desire must be awakened to abandon the previous incorrect attitude. The teacher asks the child whether he really feels happy as he is at present and whether he hasn't already thought that there might be a better way of living a happy life.

2. The trick of seeming to confirm the child's attitude. The teacher admits that from his own (erroneous) point of view the child may well be right. If, for example, he feels himself under some sort of obligation to become a thief, then he must begin practising early. At the same time, the teacher will express some doubt as to whether the child is really under any sort of obligation to develop like that.

3. The technique of apparent surrender: 'The community can put a man out of harm's way when he harms the community, but no one can force a man to be a good citizen. . . . I can only knock at the door; you are the only one who can open. . . . The key is kept inside. . . .'

4. The revelation of the Inferiority Feeling. Now we can gradually make it clear to the child that he is merely trying to deceive himself

because he is not prepared to believe in his own strength. But let him once try to face his tasks courageously, and all will be different.

This technique can be learned, though certainly not by merely trying to put abstract rules into operation. The practical methods of some expert teacher should be studied and then applied to a particular case, and the technique thus acquired should be perfected by merciless self-criticism. The cases we shall quote later will adequately demonstrate the practice of this technique.

The object of the self-realization is not only to bring the unknown to the surface, or, to continue with the metaphor previously adopted, to make the child see the invisible helmsman or controller operating within him, but to release positive forces which it will be the teacher's business thereafter to encourage methodically, so that the child becomes firmly established on the useful side of life. When we talk to the child we review his previous, fruitless attempts to master his tasks and the unsuitable means he adopted, and then we persuade him to tell us what he thinks ought to be done in the various situations in which he finds himself. To give a practical example, when we are talking to a child who is greatly inclined to exaggeration we show him that previously he has so embellished his observations that his stories have gone very near to the verge of lies. After this backward glance we proceed, more or less, in the following fashion:

'One or two children were absent from class today. Formerly you would have gone home and told your mother: "The whole class was absent today." What would you say now?' And then we leave the child to find his own way of reacting to the situation. Or the teacher will say: 'You see a funeral. Formerly you would have said: "Mother, I saw a funeral today. There were hundreds of carriages." What would you say now?' In such ways, we train him to reorientate his thought, and this training will prove very profitable with violent boys, lazy boys, obstinate boys, boys who are always playing the fool, boys who play truant, and so on.

We have likewise to train the child towards practical action and the mastering of difficulties. As Alfred Adler declared: 'If there were no difficulties for children to face we should have to invent them.' The teacher will steadily increase the demands he makes on the child. The difficulties which he gives the child to overcome are a sort of exercise apparatus on which the child must develop its own strength. It is the task of the teacher as an instructor to increase the difficulties systematically and methodically, particularly in the teaching sphere. In order to overcome difficulties in the teaching sphere we can adopt the helper system, which we have already described.

One problem in beginning the child's training towards the useful side of life lies in the fact that it is first necessary to assist the child to a success experience. The task of the teacher is to arrange situations in which the chances of such success experiences are favourable, and, if possible, in such a fashion that the child will arrive at this all-important experience of success in a natural manner.

Example: Immediately after the first talk with Arthur the teacher is correcting the work of the class. In the composition Arthur has submitted the teacher underlines a particularly good sentence. The next day he causes the three best compositions to be read out. Several of the children are allowed to read out sentences which they have written particularly well. Arthur is amongst them. The whole thing is arranged by the teacher in his role of stage-manager purely in order to give Arthur the feeling that he 'can do it, too'.

Or in a conversation Arthur tells the teacher that he once lost some money, but that later on he found it again. The teacher encourages Arthur to tell the story at great length, and in great detail. A few days later, the teacher gives as the subject of a class composition: 'But it all ended happily.' Of course, Arthur writes the story of the lost money which was found. Naturally he describes it quite well. The composition is a good one and Arthur has the honour of reading it out to the class. He has his success experience.

Or: the teacher says to the mother in an interview: 'I know that Arthur likes reading. I am going to give him a book to read: *Robinson Crusoe*. You start reading it and letting him see that you find it very interesting. When Arthur asks you for it let him have it.' A few days later the mother reports: 'I read it in the evening and he asked for it at once, but I said that I must read it through first because it was so interesting. He asked me once or twice for the book after that and then I gave it to him.'

Soon after the teacher brings the talk in the class around to savages, and he asks whether perhaps anyone has read *Robinson Crusoe*. Arthur immediately says that he has and tells the class all about the book. He has achieved his success experience. In the break, the teacher observes that quite a number of the other boys have gathered round Arthur to find out more about the book, and that Arthur is talking to them very animatedly.

CHAPTER IX

The Case of Theodore

*

The children have passed from the elementary school to the secondary school. On their third day we give them a test dictation to discover the general level of orthography. In correcting the work the teacher has a shock. Theodore has made no less than thirty-eight mistakes in spelling. His work is far below the average level of the class, and that in itself is a warning signal for the teacher.

Theodore is a weakly, weedy, pale-faced child. His stance is bad, and his movements are noticeably clumsy. His speech is adenoidal and his pronunciation is very unclear. An interview with his mother provides the following picture:

The father is an assistant carpenter and earns between thirty and thirty-five Austrian shillings weekly, but he is often out of work. The mother earns a little by ironing, but this income is irregular. The home consists of one room and a kitchen. The mother describes her husband as a man who pays little attention to the child and is satisfied when he is not bothered by the boy. When Theodore is a nuisance the father loses his temper and is quick with a blow. The father's upbringing of the child is confined almost entirely to forbidding him to play on the street—'because he would only learn bad ways there'. This opinion is, it appears, shared by the mother. When the father is at home the child spends most of his time with the mother. When the teacher observes that the father's standpoint seems to be: 'It doesn't matter what happens as long as I'm left in peace'—the mother agrees at once. She also says that her husband doesn't like meeting people, keeps himself to himself, has no friends, and only one hobby: fishing.

Theodore has a sister who is twelve years older. We shall have

The Case of Theodore

something to say about her later. The mother, who speaks bad German, is, on the whole, rather obsequious. Whatever the teacher says is right. She is willing, but things have to be put as simply as possible if she is to understand them.

From the discussion with her we gain some picture of Theodore's development. He was born under quite normal circumstances, but he was weakly from the beginning and, as an infant, he caused a good deal of trouble. He always wanted to be carried, for example. The father never had any proper relationship with the child, and the older child, the daughter, also paid very little attention to him. As a small child he was left very much to himself because the mother had to go out to work. She used to lock him in the house alone when she went out. The first time she did this he howled pitifully but, after a while, he got used to it and amused himself with bricks and so on. The presence of father or sister never stopped his playing, but as soon as his mother came back he would stop. His attachment to his mother became particularly clinging when he had measles and scarlet fever. In describing the situation the mother used a very telling and graphic expression: 'I was just like a pendulum swinging from kitchen to living-room.' When the teacher observed how appropriate this descriptive phrase was the mother became a little embarrassed, but then began to talk with touching frankness. After his bout of sickness, Theodore began to make trouble again about being left alone when his mother went out to work, but far more vehemently than before. As the scenes he created grew more and more violent the mother looked around for some other kind of work and began to take in washing to iron at home. Theodore was triumphant: his mother was now with him all the time.

At this point the sister began to play a more decisive role in the household. She was now almost seventeen and worked as an ironer in a laundry. She had picked up with a man of whom her mother did not approve and, in consequence, the situation at home changed for the worse, and bickering and quarrelling became frequent. The sister became aggressive, declared that she earned her own living and was not going to be interfered with. The father shouted and the mother wept. Theodore exploited the situation to the utmost, supported his mother zealously against his 'nasty' sister, asked his mother repeatedly why she was crying and did his best to console her. At this time he even succeeded in securing permission to sleep in his mother's bed.

123

His attachment to his mother became closer and closer. The more she became estranged from her daughter the more she turned to Theodore, who helped her, flattered her, loved her, was no worry to her, and who would certainly, in her opinion, turn out very differently one day from the wayward daughter.

But it was now time for Theodore to go to school. He did very badly. For one thing, he was left-handed and found it very difficult to learn to write. His mother began to find it a problem to get him to school at all. The father was frequently out of work and it became necessary for her to earn more money than before. She asked the father to help the child with his school work, but the man had no patience and his attitude robbed the child of all confidence. When the mother had time to help the child, for instance on Sundays, things went very much better.

In his first class, Theodore's inability to spell became very noticeable. He just could not remember what he was shown again and again. In the lower class he had a teacher who showed up his failings before the class and once exposed some of his work which had been smothered with corrections in red ink as a warning example to the rest of the class. The next teacher was more understanding and Theodore got on better with him, but he was still mortally afraid of spelling. He made the same mistakes over and over again, and seemed to have great difficulty in picturing the look of words. However, somehow or the other, he managed to get through the elementary school though the complaints about his bad spelling did not cease. He had to be forced more and more to do his work at all. Very often he succeeded in dodging it. At home he amused himself, making things, and his father's toolbag was a great attraction for him.

He was unable to establish any friendly relationship with other children. Outside the school he was the typical lonely child, and in school he made few friends. His attitude towards his classmates can best be described by saying that his relations to them were merely conventional. He would talk to the others and sometimes join in the laughter, but he never made any real friends or established any firm relationship with any group.

Now let us turn to Theodore's own evidence as visible in his compositions. Here is a judgment on his parents which sprang unconsciously from his pen:

'I don't like my father because he is always very cross with me and scolds me a lot. When they go anywhere I always have to go, too. My father never lets me go anywhere and that makes me wild. But he has his good sides. He always fixes my fishing tackle so that I can catch fish like he does. In the end I get everything I want, but it takes a long time, perhaps a year. My mother is grand.'

And a few memories of his childhood:

1. 'When I was three I wanted to be a cobbler. One day I found an old pair of boots with holes in them. That was fine. I got hold of some leather, though it was only brown paper. Then I needed a bradawl and a hammer. I got my tools together so that I could start. I cut out a piece of brown paper and pasted it on to the soles and then hammered away until the paper was all torn. Later on, I wanted to be a carpenter, and I still do.'

2. How I was once afraid: When I was five years old I was very much afraid of the stork. One evening I had my eyes open. There was a couch opposite my bed. My mother's clothes were on it. On top was her skirt. The skirt looked like a stork and I screamed "Mother! Mother!" She called out to me: "What's the matter?" And I said: "There's a stork on the couch." My mother got up and showed me that it was only her skirt. Then I could go to sleep.'

3. 'In my free time I do carpentering. I make things for the house. I learned on my own how to file a key. I got hold of batteries and a bulb and I made a light over my bed. When I once went to see my uncle I said to him: "I can draw lighting circuits." And when I drew one he was very much surprised.'

4. 'My favourite lessons are physics and sums.'

5. 'Sometimes I like reading and sometimes I don't. It all depends on the book.'

We learned that Theodore sleeps badly and has disturbing dreams. Most of his dreams, which he is quite prepared to talk about, have the same basic motive: there are dangers on every hand. We shall return to this later.

The first thing to do was to establish contact with Theodore himself. The old trick of expressing appreciation for achievements which are really nothing at all out of the ordinary worked in his case, too. To walk down a corridor sedately on occasion is not a very great achievement. However, Theodore receives a word of praise on that account. The first time he looks up at the teacher in astonishment;

*praising + minor
responsibility
mistakes
ignored*

the second time he smiles in a friendly fashion. Occasionally he is given something to carry for the teacher. He is never rebuked and—pedagogue cover your face!—his mistakes are let pass without remark. A week after the first talk the mother reports: 'A miracle has happened. Theodore has been talking a lot about school and always with enthusiasm. He hasn't time to finish his breakfast properly in the morning, he's so anxious to get to school.' Right: the tricks have worked. She is pleased and astonished, and her greater willingness to talk indicates that a satisfactory contact has been established with her as well as with Theodore. Now she will be able to stand the truth. Cautiously we explain to her what we have been able to discover so far. We show her that we quite understand her own difficult situation, and that we certainly recognize her good intentions. Then we explain to her as simply and clearly as possible how the peculiarities of the child have developed.

Our first two talks with the child are harmless chats about himself and his life. He expresses his readiness to write two compositions. The one, 'How I was once afraid,' which we have already quoted, and 'How I once exploded with rage'. Two days later he brings the two compositions and another one he has written:

'When I was five years old I had a bed with rails. One Sunday I was very bad. At midnight I was dreaming everything and I tried to climb over the rails of my bed to get to my mother. My mother heard the noise and woke up. She got a shock, took me and put me down again.'

The following conversation developed from this composition:

Teacher: 'When you were little did you always want to crawl into your mother's bed?'

Theodore: 'Yes, because I was afraid.'

Teacher: 'Perhaps it was really the other way round: you were afraid because you wanted to crawl into your mother's bed. You loved your mother very much and you wanted to be with her all the time. Not only during the day but at night as well. Lots of children are like that. I was the same when I was very young. Do you still want to creep into your mother's bed now?'

(The teacher was able to ask this question because he already knew from what the mother had told him that the boy no longer tried to creep into her bed.)

Theodore: 'No, not now.'

Teacher: 'Well, of course, when you're in the secondary school you naturally don't want to behave like a little baby. It's quite different in the secondary school, isn't it? How did you get on in the elementary school, by the way?'

The teacher now begins to talk about Theodore's bad performance in spelling. Theodore told about his former teacher, and tears came into his eyes.

Teacher: 'Yes, I can imagine that you felt hurt. I'm sure that if that had happened to me I should always have been afraid of the spelling lesson, and then because I was afraid I should have done everything worse than ever. That's probably what happened to you. Now I begin to understand how it comes about that you make so many mistakes in spelling. I have always seen the mistakes, of course, but up to now I've not said anything about them. First of all, I thought to myself, now there must be a reason for this; let me see if I can find out what it is. Now I know. And now you know, too. And then, secondly, there's no great hurry. We've got four years in the secondary school, and in that time you'll certainly be able to learn all you don't know now. Don't you think so?'

Theodore: 'Oh, yes!'

Teacher: 'Of course! You see, we'll soon put this spelling business into its proper place.'

The following letter was then sent to Theodore's mother:

'When you told me on your last visit that Theodore now goes willingly to school it showed me that we had succeeded in establishing sufficient contact with him to justify us taking the next step, which is to fill up some of the gaps in his knowledge, and particularly in spelling. You and I both know, and so does Theodore, that he is backward in some respects. Now we must see what can be done about it. One thing is quite certain: the school won't be able to do much without your help and therefore I should very much like to have another chat with you about how best we can begin. Would you therefore be good enough to come and see me again next Friday, so that we can discuss how best to help your boy. I am sure that we shall be able to help him, though it may prove rather difficult and require a good deal of patience.'

In discussion with the mother it was agreed that every day Theodore should copy a short composition, paying careful attention to every word, and that he should then write it out again at his mother's dictation. The mother was then to make a note of every word Theodore spelt properly. She was not to count the words which were mis-spelt, but merely to correct them. It was not possible to adopt any more complicated proceeding because the mother herself was not very good at German.

At school Theodore was given a helper to assist him. His first three school compositions after that were not corrected by the teacher at all. In the first only a very few words were properly spelt, but in the second most of them were correct. But in making a fair copy of the work in his exercise book Theodore still made mistakes. On his fourth school composition the teacher wrote:

'Make your corrections in the rough draft first. . . . I will look through it and then you can make a fair copy in your exercise book. I don't see why you should have so many mistakes. Others can do it, and so can you, don't you think? Some words which other boys often write wrongly, you write correctly. You have already made obvious progress. When you see a new word in a book, in a newspaper or on a placard, then take your pen—that will be your lance—and spear it. You must be like a hunter. You must think to yourself: "Every properly written word is mine. I'll spear it straight away and add it to my collection." And all the words in your collection will be the words you can spell properly.'

Soon after that the teacher wrote in Theodore's book:

'Count how many words you have already spelt correctly in your school work. And then count how many you have mis-spelt. You will be astonished to find out how much you have already learnt. In what I am now writing there will probably be new words to interest you. Spear them straight away. Put them in your collection. Other children collect butterflies and beetles. You can collect words.'

After the sixth composition Theodore wrote down his own comment: 'I know it could be better, but I am glad that it is already as good as it is.'

The teacher wrote underneath: 'You are glad and I am glad.'

In the course of seven months there was a very big change in Theodore. Not only in his spelling, but also in his general attitude to the community. Without any special encouragement his manner had become freer and more open and he had made one or two friends. His relationship with the boy who had been appointed his helper was particularly close.

A dream afforded a good insight into his mental state. 'We went to sleep peacefully. After a while I heard a noise. What could it be? The window frame fell down and I got up and looked out. There were flames everywhere and not a fireman in sight. I began to be afraid, but I didn't let that stop me. I took a bucket full of water and poured it on the fire. It was no good and I called out "Mother! Mother!" And my mother woke me up.'

The teacher wrote under this description: 'Do you understand this dream? I will try to explain it to you. You went to sleep peacefully. That means you had nothing to worry you. You go to school willingly because you know you can do things now. After a while there was a noise. That meant that you were still making mistakes. The window frame fell down. That meant that your hopes of becoming a good scholar had collapsed. There was no fireman in sight. That meant that there was no one there to help you. But you write: "I began to be afraid, but I didn't let that stop me." That means that now you don't lose courage altogether. You took a bucket full of water, and tried to put out the fire. You called out for your mother; that means you would like her to help you. I think you will understand your dream now. You are not yet quite certain that you will be able to learn everything. You still have doubts. Not during the day, of course, because then you drive all doubt away, but in the night the doubt comes up again. And then you dream such dreams. But really, there is nothing to worry about. You are making excellent progress, and you will quite certainly learn the rest of the spelling.'

A couple of weeks later Theodore wrote down the following dream he had had:

'I went to sleep. Suddenly I heard a growling. I looked round. There was a lion standing next to me, but the funny thing was the lion was tame. When I turned round he roared at me. I looked around me more carefully. I was surrounded by four walls. The lion looked into my eyes in a friendly fashion. A lioness wanted to maul me, but he wouldn't let her. There was no need for me to be frightened. One after another more lions jumped in. And then I heard my mother calling me softly and I woke up.'

This dream—which surely requires no particular analysis—was also discussed with the child. The main stress was still laid on his excessive attachment to his mother. A little while after that Theodore went away on holiday. In the following year, and the year after that, the teacher continued his efforts. The result was that Theodore settled down very well and his spelling improved considerably. In the third year he was turning out work in which there were perhaps only five or six mistakes of a minor nature.

CHAPTER X

The Case of Willy

Only a few years ago the psychological world had fallen a complete victim to the 'Talent nonsense' (Adler). Tests were proposed to discover exactly what kind of talent a child possessed and to what degree. When the terrible debacle of world war made it necessary to build up our devastated civilization again and the slogan 'Make way for the talented' arose, this investigation of talent led to that deplorable excess known as the 'Talent Class'. Today the practice of picking out the talented is declining, and that is due in no small measure to the results obtained by Individual Psychology, which declares roundly that every performance can be understood as a matter of training and that this training depends upon courage.

Individual Psychology regards all psychological manifestations as being directed to some particular aim. In this way it has greatly advanced the psychological understanding of laziness, stupidity and talent. Laziness, stupidity and talent are not given things which are unchangeable. They have a specific 'aim', and they must be regarded dynamically. The personality as a whole and its aims are the important thing. Our approach to the problem must therefore be in the form of a question: what is the meaning of laziness, stupidity and talent in relation to the personality (or 'aim') as a whole? This typical Individual Psychological approach is of fundamental importance. Whoever merely asks: 'Why is this child lazy, stupid or untalented?' inevitably finds himself hopelessly bogged down amidst somatic conditions almost impossible to alter. In a despairing attempt to find some answer to his question he talks about 'heredity', 'the destruction of motor centres', 'gland secretions' and so on. But when Individual Psychology asks instead, 'What is the sense or aim of stupidity, laziness and talent in the general life style of the child?' the answer comes readily enough: 'the mistaken search for security on the part of a discouraged human being fearful of defeats on the useful side of life'. This answer provides us with our 'educational jumping-off point'. Mistakes can be exposed. Mistakes can be corrected.

With this we have come to the heart of the matter. If we want to turn laziness into industry and lack of talent into talent, then first of all we must try to understand the mistaken outlook of the child; we must try to discover the point at which the child's mistake began. From the material that we obtain by observation and inquiry we must show the child how his original mistake developed. At the same time we must make it clear that we are not condemning him, and in this way we shall bring him relief. We must then encourage him to take the first hesitant steps towards the useful side of life. We must use our whole bag of tricks to bring him to his first success experience. At the same time we must secure the assistance of his parents and of the other teachers in the process of re-education. By systematic training we must establish the child firmly on his feet. We must teach the child to see the motives of his own attempts at escape, thus helping him to educate himself and obviating any excessive self-love. All this involves a great deal more than those innocents imagine who think that the system of Individual Psychology consists in saying to a child: 'You are already a big boy now and things are improving.'

Let us now take a concrete example. After four years in the elementary school, Willy came into the secondary school. It is not long before he makes his presence disagreeably felt. First of all, in relation to discipline. He usually finds something to fiddle with in class and he very seldom pays any attention to what the teacher is saying. It may be the strap of his satchel which interests him, and this he rolls carefully round and round his finger and then lets it spiral off again. Or he will fiddle endlessly with a cheap fountain pen he possesses and of which he is inordinately proud. He will screw and unscrew the top again and again. He will fill and empty it repeatedly. Perhaps in doing so he makes an ink blot or two, then the cleaning up of the blots involves further long and wearisome manipulations. Called to attention by the teacher and told to get on with his work he will look up with injured astonishment, as much as to say: 'Really! Can't you see I'm busy. I've got to clean up these ink blots. Aren't you for ever telling us that we ought to be neat and tidy?'

On another occasion he will perhaps work away as though hypnotized on a piece of paper which he is endeavouring to turn into a star. A remark of the teacher is just ignored, and at last the star is completed. Then he spits on it and tries to fasten it to his jacket. The amusement of the other boys at his never-ending antics can be imagined. There's hardly a dull moment when Willy is around—but the lessons suffer. Or perhaps on other occasions Willy will just stare out of the window, condescending to give the teacher his attention only infrequently. If the teacher dares to address him a second time he immediately feels insulted and withdraws his attention and the circus can then begin again. After a while things quieten down, but there is no question of any further attention to the rest of the lesson.

As soon as the bell rings for the break Willy comes to life again. He climbs on his desk, shouts at the top of his voice and makes faces —something he often does during lessons as well, particularly if a neighbour happens to nudge him to draw him gently to attention. And often he sticks out his tongue for inspection. In the break he is tireless at inventing new tricks. In particular he loves playing the clown, and the circus in general is the object of his passionate enthusiasm. For him a ruler is just something to balance on his nose. The tip-seats in the lavatory provide him with an endless source of fun. Needless to say, he is always surrounded by a group of noisy boys who reward his fooling with roars of laughter and urge him on to ever more extraordinary performances. But when the bell goes and lessons begin again he sinks into himself like a heap of ashes when the fire has gone out—or starts fiddling once again with the strap of his satchel. . . .

His school work is, as might be expected, very unsatisfactory. He takes no positive and useful part in the class discussions. His observation is extremely superficial and inaccurate. He makes notes of very little and his ability to recollect things is very poor. His compositions occasionally show a good turn of phrase, but on the whole, they are unsatisfactory and full of mistakes. One thing in particular is very noticeable: causal relationships are a mystery to him. He is unable to understand cause and effect, and often quite incapable of drawing the simplest conclusions. In the geography lesson, for example, we have discussed the problem of silting and erosion at some length. The children establish the fact that water carries stones, sand and mud along with it, and learn about alluvial deposits. One of the boys mentioned: 'I was once on a Danube steamer, and near Korneuberg one of the sailors said to my father, "There's another new sandbank formed there." '

Teacher: 'So a new sandbank had formed suddenly in the Danube. Now imagine a steamer sailing along. The captain and the helmsman know nothing about this new sandbank. What might easily happen? What do you think, Willy?'

Willy has no idea. Now the teacher—who has great difficulty in preventing other boys from answering for Willy—sketches the situation on the blackboard. In the picture the bows of the vessel are going straight towards the sandbank.

'Well, Willy, what do you think might happen?'

Willy still doesn't answer, and then one of the other boys, unable to suppress his impatience any longer, bursts out with the obvious answer. The teacher then remarks: 'What a pity. You took the words out of his mouth. He was just going to say it.' (Incidentally, a trick that can often be used to make defeat less painful for children.)

The boy's inability to think logically showed above all—as one might expect from the nature of things—in mathematics. Sums lay in another and strange world as far as Willy was concerned. His ignorance of the multiplication table was almost disarming. At the utmost, he was able to do mechanical additions successfully. The quality of his work in general made his removal to a higher class at the end of the year highly problematical. Willy was a cut-and-dried candidate for ploughing.

Our first talk with him took place outside the class. A message was sent: 'Will Willy please come to Mr. X's room.' Willy was thus called out of another class in the middle of a lesson. Perhaps a schoolmaster of the old type would turn pale at this, but we knew what we were after. We desired to create a certain tension. When Willy arrived the tension was increased by the fact that at first we paid no attention to him but continued writing. Only after a while did we give him our full attention.

Teacher: 'I have just been revising your school questionnaire and I wanted to tell you that I urgently needed your birth certificate. Please bring it along tomorrow without fail.'

Willy nods.

The Case of Willy

Teacher (lighting a cigarette in order to dissipate the school atmosphere and speaking in a friendly tone): 'Well, how do you like it in school?'

Willy: 'It's not so bad.'

Teacher: 'Good. It's really not so bad, is it? Quite agreeable, in fact. Even amusing. Where would you sooner be, by the way, at school or at home?'

Willy (without hesitation): 'At school.'

The decisive fashion in which this preference is expressed arouses our interest. So he would much prefer to be at school? A certain suspicion begins to take shape. When anyone, whether child or adult, expresses an opinion so decidedly against his home then it is reasonable to assume that for some reason or other he does not feel very comfortable at home. We begin to wonder what is wrong at home, and we decide to follow up our first clue.

Teacher: 'Oh! Why's that?'

Willy: 'It's dull at home.'

Teacher: 'Are you alone at home?'

Willy: 'No.'

This curt answer and the aversion in the tone strengthen our suspicion that between Willy and someone whom for the moment we must refer to as X there is considerable tension. In any case, it is obvious that the child has adopted a bellicose attitude. Against whom?

Teacher: 'So it's dull, is it?'

Willy: 'Yes.'

Once again the tone is curt and off-hand. Willy does not want to talk about his home.

Teacher: 'Have you any brothers or sisters?'

Willy: 'Yes. Five.'

Once again there is that undertone of hostility. Individual Psychology knows how important the relations between brothers and sisters can be in the development of each individual child and it never omits to investigate the situation from this angle.

Teacher: 'How old are they?'

Willy: 'The oldest is twenty-eight already. He's in Innsbruck.'

Here the tone has changed. It is less strained. There is a suggestion of pleasure. The teacher takes a chance.

Teacher: 'Oh! So he's earning his own living. And perhaps he sends home nice things for you occasionally?'

134

The expression has grown less suspicious. Willy is even grinning a little.

Teacher: 'Any other brothers?'

Willy: 'One—he's eighteen.'

Teacher: 'And the others?'

Willy: 'Then I've got three sisters.'

Teacher: 'And what about them?'

Willy: 'One of them is a tailoress and the other works in a jewellers".

The teacher waits expectantly, but Willy says nothing more. Why does he so demonstratively say nothing of the third sister? This is obviously a deliberate error. Where such striking forgetfulness is concerned, Individual Psychology is inclined to suspect that there must be something wrong with the individual's relationship to the community. Willy is the youngest in the family, and so the omitted sister is the one who comes immediately before him in the chronological order. Is this sister perhaps the reason why the life style which Willy has acquired has developed in the way it has done?

Teacher: 'And what about the youngest?'

The word 'youngest' is quite enough and already the face of Willy is set hard, the friendliness has disappeared. The head lowers and the answer comes without expression.

'She goes to a grammar school. She's thirteen.'

And the teacher observes that the right hand is clenched into a fist. A further suspicion arises. We know that the father is a jobbing tailor. Four children are still at home. The clothing suggests poverty. And yet in such a family one of the children is studying! The girl must be a good scholar. That might explain the poor performance of Willy. Very likely this sister is favoured in other respects. The affair is still very vague, but at least the teacher has discovered something that looks as though it is worth following up.

Teacher: 'What sort of a student is your sister?'

Willy: 'A very good one.'

Teacher: 'How do you know that?'

Willy: 'Mother's always saying so, and her teachers tell mother so when she goes to see them.'

Teacher: 'What class is your sister in?'

Willy: 'The second.'

This seems to be the nigger in the wood pile. Willy is a child whose way is blocked by a sister. This sister is a good scholar and apparently a favoured child. We begin to imagine what it is like at home. How the mother talks to Willy. Or is it the father, perhaps?

Teacher: 'Your father is a tailor, isn't he?'

Willy: 'Yes.'

Teacher: 'Is he strict with you?'

This question produces a broad grin.

Willy: 'Oh! No! He often gives me money.'

Teacher: 'And I suppose your mother very often doesn't know anything about it, eh?'

Willy nods gleefully. But we are not so happy about it. If a father secretly gives a child money then it is not going too far to suspect that the father himself feels that he owes the boy something, that there is something to make good to him. In any case, in the family of Willy it begins to look as though the father doesn't wear the trousers. So perhaps it's the mother who. . . .

Teacher: 'And what about your mother?'

The effect of this question is striking. The head drops again, the mouth curls, the eyes grow bright with tears and the answer comes haltingly:

'She often hits me.'

So there we are! It is now not difficult for the teacher to imagine what sort of life Willy leads at home. 'Lisa! Now, she's different. There's a child who's no trouble and gives real pleasure. She learns her lessons and all her teachers praise her. But as for you, you lazy good-for-nothing, you'll never be any good. All you do is traipse about the streets and pull silly faces. Why don't you take your sister for an example? Why can she do her lessons so well and you. . . .' And so on.

Now we can begin to interpret the case of Willy, though still with caution. Willy is not a child who merely thinks he is being pushed into the background unfairly, but this is actually the case. His more capable sister has blocked his path for years. With his own achievements denigrated, Willy has lost his courage in the effort to master the problem of school. In order to compensate for the inferiority feeling which results he seeks escape on the useless side of life, he escapes into the world of fantasy. Because he has lost his belief in his capacity for positive performance, he strives to retain at least the appearance of some prestige in the eyes of others by constantly playing the fool. How difficult his world would be if he did not at least earn the laughter and admiration of his schoolfellows by his antics! How would he be able to stand his world at all if there were not a few of his schoolfellows who favoured him because he had given them a good deal of amusement and they remembered it thankfully?

'When I get home it'll start up again,' he probably thinks to himself, 'but at school I'm a somebody. Tomorrow I'll stick a piece of paper on someone's back. Let them run to the teacher when they find out. I don't care. The others will laugh.'

If anyone thinks we are imagining things and interpreting the facts to suit ourselves let him read the compositions Willy writes:

'If I had a magic wand! If I had I would make myself into the strongest, the merriest and the cleverest person in the world. I would make a villa on a hill. I would turn myself into a fish and swim around in a big pond. If I wanted to be a bird I should turn myself into one and fly to America all amongst the negroes and then I would turn myself into a negro chief. What things I would do! I would always be the cleverest, and I'd always travel around in foreign countries. I'd go to India and Brazil, and with the steamer to America and many, many other countries. That would be fine.'

(In order to prevent all misunderstandings let it be pointed out that this composition is quoted according to the fair copy made by Willy after correcting the original draft.)

Isn't this composition enough to show that Willy is living his life in a world of fantasy? Isn't it enough to show that he is anxious to run away from a situation, at home, which he is beginning to find intolerable?

He sees his own situation only through the spectacles which the feeling of being neglected in favour of his sister has placed on his nose. His composition shows this clearly:

'My sister. My sister's name is Lisa. She is a year older than I am. I don't get on well with her. She is cunning and deceitful. Everything I have she wants. When she can't have it she starts quarrelling. If I play with her she always starts a quarrel. Nothing suits her and she's always got to have everything her own way. If I say: "This is the way to do it," she immediately says it isn't. The first time I don't take any notice, but if she keeps on I go for her. If she doesn't stop then I give her a clout. And then she says at once: "I'll tell mother! She'll thrash you silly. But you're silly already. You've even got to stay on in the same class." And when my mother comes home she starts telling tales. Often when she's done something she blames it on me and I get punished for it, and very often I don't know why I'm being hit. And sometimes she takes my school things away and when I look for them I can't find them. But she's in hospital for a week and I've got some peace. But when she comes out it will start all over again. My other sister isn't so greedy. When she has anything she gives me a bit of it.'

The general error of this child is that he thinks: 'I am unfairly treated. My mother doesn't love me much. I'm not so clever as my sister. The only thing I can do is to play the fool in school. If I don't I'm nothing at all, just dirt. I have given up all hope of ever competing with my sister or my fellow pupils at school. I shall never be any good.'

We have now put ourselves into the world of this child and tried to see things through his spectacles, so much so, that we are already beginning to think: if we were in his place should we be so very different? We have already recognized the aim which guides his behaviour: 'Attract attention or otherwise you'll count for nothing!' At the same time we have done much more than merely to place him in a category: 'discouraged child'. We have understood his discouragement against the background of his specific situation. Willy is certainly only one of a thousand cases of discouraged children but at the same time his case with all its nuances is unique; it will never recur again in quite the same way.

Opponents of Individual Psychology often say contemptuously that all children who are awkward and make difficulties are just discouraged children for the Individual Psychologists. We reply that it is high time that they realized that the important thing is not to discover merely that a child is discouraged, but to 'understand' the discouragement against the child's specific background. Individual Psychology regards the general term 'discouraged child' as a formula which can be filled with a thousandfold variety of contents. The important thing for us is not just to discover that a child is discouraged but to discover just how and in what particular form he is discouraged.

Much the same is true of another objection: 'Oh! Once you've heard the Individual Psychologists interpret a few cases you've learned the whole bag of tricks, and all you get then is the same thing over and over again.' Just the opposite is true! Each case is different provided that one seeks to understand the living individual in question and one is not easily satisfied with mouthing a few unavoidable technical terms. Does anyone refuse to read novels on the ground: 'Oh, they're all about love!' It is certainly true that most of them are about love, in some form or other, but people go on reading novels because it is not merely a question of 'love', but of the specific circumstances involved as the conflict moves towards its solution. And with a problem child the great point is to understand him in all his uniqueness, because that understanding is the preliminary to an attempt to change him. The teacher is never faced with the problem of changing 'the problem child', but of changing a particular problem child entrusted to his care. The measures he adopts to attain this desirable end will depend entirely on the specific form of discouragement he finds, and on the specific situation of the child.

Individual Psychology is anxious to treat the cause of a difficulty, and not its outward symptoms. That is something the reader must always keep in mind when he notices that we do not spend much time talking about the pranks worked up by Willy. They are mere symptoms. We therefore go straight on with the discussion of what we regard as fundamental.

Teacher: 'How does your sister do in mathematics?'

Willy: 'She gets a "very good".'

Teacher: 'And what did you get in the elementary school?'

Willy: 'Sufficient.'

Teacher: 'Well, in that case I'm not surprised that you always think that your sister is cleverer than you are. If my brother, who is also older than I, always got a "good" when I only got a "poor" then very likely I should have got the idea that he was cleverer than I. You still believe that your sister is cleverer, more hard-working and better behaved than you are, don't you?'

At this point, Willy turns away. He has been touched on his most vulnerable spot.

Teacher: 'And then when you get the strap it's small wonder that you begin to think that no one cares for you much.'

Willy begins to cry.

Teacher: 'Don't cry. Even if it really has been like that, that doesn't mean to say it's got to stay like it, you know. I'll tell you what, I want to help you make it different. We can't do anything about the fact that your sister can do more than you can—after all, she's older than you are, and she's already in a higher class. There's no virtue in being older. When you are as old as she is . . . let me see . . . you'll be in the third class then. Won't you know more than she does now in the second?'

The Case of Willy

Willy: 'Oh, yes!'

Teacher: 'Well, there you are! Tell me, do you get any pleasure out of learning things?'

Willy: 'Oh, yes!'

Teacher: 'That's good. After all, you're getting a big fellow and you're already in the middle school like your sister. This is a sort of middle school, too, you know. But I think that up to now you have been a bit afraid of sums and, in fact, of the school in general.'

Willy: 'Oh, no!'

Teacher: 'I don't mean afraid in the way you do. I know that you weren't afraid the teacher was going to beat you. What I mean is that you were afraid of learning because you thought you wouldn't be able to do anything worth while at it. You thought to yourself: "No, I'll never be able to do what my sister can do, so what's the use of trying." I can imagine just how you felt. But I'm sure you were wrong. I don't believe your sister is so very much cleverer than you are. In fact, I'm certain you can be every bit as clever as she is. Why not? But you didn't believe that, and that's just where you went wrong. What your sister can do, you can do, too.'

That was quite enough for one day. We have taken Willy by surprise and let him see clearly how much we have already discovered about him. When the time came to leave the room, Willy hesitated. Had he already felt the human warmth which lay in the teacher's words?

The next step was to talk to his mother. At the invitation of the teacher she appeared at the school. She turned out to be a typical Viennese housewife. She put down her shopping bag carefully and sat down with a certain amount of circumspection. It was easy enough to see from her attitude that for her a teacher was a person to be treated with respect. The first thing to do was to find the right contact with her. A few friendly words and a little familiar Viennese dialect helped, and then she started off:

'Well, teacher, what's he been up to now? He's a little devil. You have no idea what a burden that child is to me. He just won't learn. I might have given up in despair long ago if my youngest daughter weren't such a treasure. She's just the opposite of the boy. Such a good child. Whenever I go to her school—she goes to a grammar school, you know—her teachers praise her to the skies. But the boy's just a good-for-nothing. I suppose he's just the same in school as he is at home?'

140

The Case of Willy

There was really very little more the mother could tell us. All our suspicions were confirmed at once. Our next step was to change her attitude. But, of course, it was too early to reveal to her how she came to adopt such an attitude towards the two children. All we could do for the moment was to bring her to recognize the mistake she had made. That would not be too difficult. She was the type of woman who is not easily angered. What should we say in answer to her question? Our reaction must certainly be different from what she expected.

Teacher: 'Well, I must say sometimes I've had to laugh at him myself, and I'm sure you have. He's a cheerful lad.'

Mother: 'Cheerful lad? Is he? But why does he learn so badly?'

For the moment we must agree with her. After all, there was some justification for her heart-felt sigh! It will be easier to establish contact if we seem to take her side at first—but with reservations.

Teacher: 'Yes, I can imagine what you have to put up with. But I don't think it's really necessary. . . .'

Mother: 'There you are! I've told him a hundred times: "Look at your sister. Why can she do everything and you can't? Because she works hard. That's why!" You'd hardly believe it, sir, but the moment that child comes home she sits down to her work. But the boy has to be forced into it. And the cuffs he's had!'

Teacher: 'Oh! And did that help?'

Mother: 'Not a bit. He only got worse.'

At this point we must surprise the mother and carry the war into her own country. The device has often been tried and it never fails.

Teacher: 'Tell me, Mrs. N., I'm sure you're a good cook?'

Mother (very much surprised): 'Well, yes, I suppose I'm not bad.'

Teacher: 'Well, then, try to imagine the following: You stand over the gas stove every day doing your very best to make everything as nice as possible, and then your husband comes in to his meal and he's always got something to complain of. One day he thinks you've over-salted the food. Another day it's overcooked; the next day it's under-cooked. And he's always saying: "Look at your sister! Why can't you cook like she does?" And when there's onion sauce he says to you: "Do you call that onion sauce? Why don't you ask your sister how she makes it? She can cook. It's a pity you can't take an example from her." And supposing he went on like that, day after day. If you ask me, it wouldn't be long before. . . .'

The Case of Willy

Mother (laughing despite herself): 'Yes, you're right; it wouldn't be long before I threw it at him.'

Teacher (suddenly very serious and in a more decided tone): 'Well, what about Willy then? Don't you think he feels much the same as you would?'

For a moment or two there is silence.

Teacher (in a softer voice): 'And does he get cuffs very often?'

Mother (suddenly very uncertain of herself): 'Well, only when he deserves it. . . .'

Teacher: 'Look, I'll make a suggestion. The cuffing doesn't do any good at all. Let's try something different. Frankly, I think the trouble is that the boy has lost all courage. He has lost all belief in himself. He doesn't think he could do anything if he tried. But I had a chat with him today and I think he's going to try now. Of course, you mustn't think he's going to be perfect straight away, but I think we can obtain an improvement. You must help me. Unless you do, I shan't be able to do anything on my own. When you've got more time to spare come and see me again and I'll try to explain to you how it's all come about. I think I've found out what's happened. But what are we going to do now; that's the thing. I'll tell you what: give me your word you won't hit the boy again. At least, not for the next fortnight. Not a cuff, not a push—whatever happens. Will you do it?'

Mother: 'It won't work, you'll see. He won't do anything at all.'

Teacher: 'Leave that to me. I'll make it my business to talk to him about it. Don't you worry. Now let us make a bargain, eh? You promise not to touch him for a fortnight, and not to scold him no matter what happens, and in that time I'll do my best to bring him round. Keep your part of the bargain faithfully for a fortnight, and after that if we haven't had any success, all right, you can start hitting him again. Or perhaps you won't even then. I rather imagine you feel already that blows aren't any good. And now promise me: no blows, no scoldings for a fortnight, whatever happens. Agreed?'

The mother promises and shakes the teacher's hand.

And now back to Willy. In the break after this talk with his mother he was unusually quiet. He sat at his desk and ate his sandwiches. In the next break he was again the centre of a little circle. During the lessons he was obviously doing his best and paying more attention although there were frequent moments when his attention strayed and he got up to his old tricks. Two days later he was called to the teacher's room. This time we had to make him realize the connection between his tomfoolery and his lack of success at his lessons.

Teacher: 'Ah, there you are again, Willy! You know, it looks to me as though you had become quite a different lad. I noticed the way you were paying attention the very next day. I was very pleased. During your lessons and coming to school seems to give you more pleasure now than it did. I can imagine what you're thinking: "If I really could do something worth while at school I'd be glad. But I don't think I can!" You hesitate to get up and say anything because you think: "Perhaps I shall say something silly and then the others will all laugh at me." You've often thought that, haven't you?'

Willy says nothing but nods his head.

Teacher: 'Well, I can understand that. Your sister does her lessons very well and everyone praises her. I can imagine that your mother is often saying: "Look at your sister! Look how well she does her work! Everyone's satisfied with her at school, and she never brings home any bad marks." And if you keep on hearing that you're not so good as someone else you end up by believing it. That's what's happened to you, isn't it? When I was a boy something of the sort happened to me. I couldn't understand my teacher's explanation of how you went on after subtracting, and because I didn't understand I always had a horror of the mathematics lesson. When it was my turn to stand up I was tongue-tied and couldn't say a thing right. And to make things worse, there was one boy who sat near me who laughed at me. In the break he used to put his finger to his forehead when he looked at me as much as to say, "You're not all there." Well, you can imagine how I felt! I used to wonder what I could do to show that boy a thing or two. And there were one or two others like him in my class. On our way home we had to go over a railway and it was always a great joke for us to dance about in the clouds of smoke and steam that came up when a train passed under the bridge. To impress the others I said: "You wait till the next train comes. I'll spit right down the funnel." And I did! Right into the middle. Was that a triumph for me! The next day all the class had heard about my feat, and the boy who had always laughed at me came up to me and said: "Are you going to spit down the funnel again today?" After that he didn't laugh at me any more and we became friends. So you see, your teacher did just as silly things as you do when he was a boy. All children do at some time or the other. Now why do you think I've told you that, Willy? Because I think it's just the same with you.

The Case of Willy

Isn't it true that you play the fool so much because you think it will make the other boys admire you?'

Willy says nothing and is clearly very embarrassed.

Teacher: 'We all make mistakes. It's very human. And you're making a mistake, too. You think that because you can't do your lessons very well and therefore can't be admired for that you must play the fool in the break to draw attention to yourself and make the others gather round and admire you. Perhaps people have said to you already: "You ought to be ashamed of yourself, playing the fool like that!" I'm not going to say you ought to be ashamed of yourself. Why should you be ashamed of yourself? Because you have made a mistake? No, I've already told you: everyone makes mistakes. The great thing is not to keep on making mistakes once you've realized they are mistakes. But you know, we could all learn much more in class if there weren't always a few boys who played the fool and wasted our time. That's a nuisance, don't you think?'

Willy nods his head: 'Yes!'

Teacher: 'You know, I'd like to have a few more boys in the class who realized that. Who realized that it's not really very funny to crawl about under the desks, to scrape their feet on the floor and to rush around shouting at the tops of their voices. A few boys who would help the others who haven't yet realized it and are still making their mistakes, who would talk to them in the break and encourage them to do something else instead. Do you think you could do that, for example?'

Willy (eagerly): 'Oh, yes!'

Teacher: 'Well, why not try it then? I think you could, too.'

Whilst speaking, the teacher took both the boy's hands in his own. Willy beamed and then suddenly raised the teacher's hands and put them against his cheeks. Is there any need for further proof that Willy is one of those children who feel that they are pushed into the background in favour of brothers or sisters and who long for a little warmth and friendship?

At the end of a week the mother comes to see the teacher without being asked. After a general chat the core of the matter is reached.

Teacher: 'And so, you see, that's what happens to anyone who loses confidence in himself. You meant well, I know. I never doubted that. You wouldn't have been a real mother if you hadn't felt hurt when one of your children did badly at school. And then, of course, you constantly held up the sister as an example. I can understand

144

that, too. But the boy couldn't. He got it into his head that he just couldn't do anything right at school and particularly not his sums. And so he began to play the fool. I can well imagine that you often talked yourself hoarse to him.'

(At this point the mother went off into a very graphic description of how, in fact, she had talked herself hoarse in an attempt to get the boy to do his work properly, but there was nothing new in the tale for us.)

Teacher: 'There you are. But you see, it did no good at all because the boy was firmly convinced that you loved his sister more than you did him. I can almost imagine that the thing did Lisa no good either. She would hardly be human if she weren't just a little bit vain about her own cleverness. Isn't she perhaps just a little bit—what shall we say, cocky?'

Mother: 'Oh, no! Perhaps she does let you know a bit that she's a good scholar, but. . . .'

Teacher: 'But it wouldn't need much to give her just a little swelled head. And then that would be bad for Lisa, too. You wouldn't want that, would you? But what about Willy again? Don't you think he has changed a little recently?'

Mother: 'Well, he's not so quarrelsome, I must admit that.'

Teacher: 'I think it wouldn't do any harm if you just happened to remark about it to him. Why not say something like: "I don't know how it is, Willy, but you seem to have changed lately. You seem much better than you were." He's got to see that you notice his efforts to be different.'

With this, my notes on the case come to an end. But from memory I can add: Similar attempts at influencing the boy were necessary from time to time when difficulties arose. But gradually the difficulties subsided. In the course of years Willy completely abandoned his tomfooleries though he always remained a cheerful lad. His work improved noticeably and every year he got his remove into the next higher class. Finally he left school and the 'Below average talent' boy earned a 'good' in arithmetic.

Willy became an apprentice and conducted himself to the satisfaction of everyone.

If anyone now feels inclined to say, 'Ah, yes, but Willy was in reality talented all the time—his talent was dormant—and the treatment merely removed the obstacles and let the talent show itself,' we shall answer, 'We have no desire to quarrel with you; instead we invite you to do the same as we do and to seek, with the methods of Individual Psychology, to change the erroneous life style of a child and thus to assist his "dormant" talent to express itself.'

CHAPTER XI

The Case of Frank

The case we are now to record is, in many respects, a classic one. First of all, it confirms the view of Individual Psychology that a symptom can be explained only in its general context. A person is a whole, and every part-component becomes comprehensible only in relation to the whole. Secondly, it shows how the therapy of Individual Psychology exerts influence not merely on the symptom or symptoms, but on the root cause and at the spot where the child— giving way to the erroneous belief that he is unable to master the tasks set him by life—has branched off into the training of a neurotic life style. Above all, the therapy of Individual Psychology reveals how the child came to set his eyes on a fictitious aim and let this fateful action be 'followed by the consequences'. And finally, the case is interesting because at one point it gives us a clear insight into *how* the self-realization of what was previously operating in the child without his knowledge, is brought about.

On 1st December 19 . . . shortly before the end of the break, I made the acquaintance of the mother when she came to inquire how her boy was getting on.

Teacher: 'There is nothing in particular which strikes one about the boy. He is rather quiet and serious and, on the whole, his work is satisfactory.'

Mother (suddenly bursting into tears): 'The worry I have with that child! I'm at my wits' end. I don't know what to do with him.'

Teacher: 'What's wrong with the boy? Has he done anything in particular which worries you?' (The mother is now sobbing without restraint.) 'Have you received a bad report about the boy from anyone else?' (She shakes her head.) 'Is anything wrong with him at home?'

Mother: 'He started it again last night. I don't know what to do any more. He screams in the night, and it's getting worse instead of better.' (With an expression of desperate anxiety.) 'I'm always afraid the boy will go mad. Is that possible? Can a child go mad?'

As I have to go off to take the class I console her as well as I can:

'Yes, I can quite understand that you're upset about it, but don't let it worry you too much. I expect we shall be able to do something. Come and see me again tomorrow. I shall have more time then.'

The next day the mother appeared again.

Teacher: 'Now, tell me what's wrong with the boy?'

Mother: 'I am really growing desperate. He did it again last night.'

Teacher: 'Tell me about it in detail.'

Mother: 'He sleeps with his sister.'

Teacher: 'How old is his sister?'

Mother: 'Nineteen.'

Teacher: 'And how old is he?'

Mother: 'Twelve. She doesn't want to sleep with him any more, because she's afraid. And it is horrible. He writhes violently in bed and then suddenly he starts screaming and throws off all the bed-clothes and goes on screaming as though someone were murdering him. And he goes absolutely white, trembles violently and screams at the top of his voice. Do you think he's going mad?'

Teacher: 'No, I certainly don't. You need not worry on that score.'

Mother: 'Two doctors have already told me that. They say it will get better when he's older. But it's terrible now. My daughter's afraid of him. It is uncanny when he opens his eyes wide and trembles over his whole body. He makes movements with his hands. It's like a convulsion. And afterwards he doesn't know anything about it. I lie in the next room always, listening, because I know by now when the fit is coming on. At first he begins to groan and I run into their room because it starts off at once after that.'

Teacher: 'Tell me: are there times when he does it less often, and other times when he does it more often perhaps?'

Mother: 'It happens mostly when something or other is going round in his head.'

The Case of Frank

Teacher: 'And do you know, by any chance, what that something is?'

Mother: 'Yes, for instance, when he gets a bad mark at school or when he knows there's homework to do. It's particularly bad then. And then he reads a lot. He reads such exciting things and I think that's what it comes from. I've often forbidden him to read such things. But it's no use. He exchanges the books secretly with other boys.'

Teacher: 'Is he easily frightened?'

Mother: 'Yes, very much so. If we're all in the kitchen he won't venture into the other room at all unless the light is first switched on. He says it's because he can't see, but it's really because he's frightened of the dark.'

Teacher: 'Was he always easily frightened? Right from the beginning? As a very young child?'

Mother: 'No. It's only since he's been going to school that he's seemed so frightened.'

Teacher: 'I have looked through his school records and I see that he wasn't a particularly good pupil. He had great difficulty in particular with arithmetic.'

Mother: 'Yes, learning anything was always a great burden for him. In the last class he almost had to stay behind.'

Teacher: 'Are there any younger brothers or sisters?'

Mother: 'Yes, a brother six years younger, and my youngest, a girl of three.'

Teacher: 'So the younger brother was born just when Frank started going to school, and his sister was born just when he came into the last class; is that right?'

Mother (after a little thought): 'Yes, that's right.'

Teacher: 'Now tell me, how does Frank get on with your other children?'

Mother: 'He gets on well with my eldest, but there, she's like a second mother to him. She's always giving him something or the other. But he's jealous of his brother and he squabbles with him over the least thing. In fact, he does little else all day but quarrel with the younger one. He's always afraid that he's missing something. If the younger boy so much as touches any of his things, it starts. I could spend all my time settling their quarrels.'

Teacher: 'And how is he with the little girl?'

Mother: 'He doesn't squabble much with her, and he looks after her quite nicely. But with his brother....'

149

The Case of Frank

Teacher: 'And what does he do when he's not squabbling with his younger brother?'

Mother: 'Reading or hanging around. I can't do anything with him. We've got a little business with the garden, rabbits and chickens, you know. But he won't do a thing to help. Do you know what he often says? "What have I got to live for? I don't like living much." What a way for a child to talk! I sometimes thing he isn't all there. And yet I give him everything I think he wants, everything he likes. But that doesn't help. He wants everything. Do you think anything can be done. . . .?'

Teacher: 'I can't promise, of course, but I think I have a fair idea of what it's all about. Come and see me again in a week or ten days.'

That same day I had the boy sent for. First of all, I had to decide cautiously how far I could go. I chatted with the lad about nothing in particular for some time and then I touched on what was in my mind.

Teacher: 'So you can't remember your first day at school very well? Can you remember what it was like before you went to school?'

Frank: 'I was in the country and I fell into the water and I shivered with cold.'

Teacher: 'Can you remember anything even earlier than that?'

Frank remains silent.

Teacher: 'Think it over carefully. Something or the other will occur to you, I'm sure.'

Frank (after a long pause): 'I was in the country. A woman gave me a sausage and the dog in our house snapped it away from me and ate it up.'

Teacher: 'And you didn't have any of the sausage! Well, it often happens that one person takes a thing away from another person. Tell me: have you any brothers or sisters?'

Frank: 'A sister.'

Teacher: 'And how old is she?'

Frank: 'Nineteen.'

Teacher: 'And you have a brother, too, haven't you?'

Frank: 'Yes.'

Teacher: 'And how old is he?'

Frank: 'He's six, and there's a little girl of three.'

Teacher: 'And do they take anything away from you?'

Frank: 'No.'

Teacher: 'But sometimes you think you're not getting your share, don't you?'

Frank remains silent.

Teacher: 'Can you remember how it was when your brother was born?'

Frank (after some hesitation): 'Mother was in a hospital for a while, and then she came home and my brother was there.'

Teacher: 'And can you remember what you thought about it?'

Frank (again after some hesitation): 'I thought: "Now I've got a brother." '

Teacher: 'And when your little sister was born? Was your mother in hospital then, too?'

Frank: 'Yes.'

Teacher: 'And when she came home the little sister was there. And what did you think then?'

Frank: 'I thought: "What do we need a sister for?" '

Teacher: 'So I suppose you weren't altogether pleased about it? But I expect you're glad now that you've got a sister; for instance, a big sister with whom you can sleep at night and not be frightened when you dream anything nasty. Do you sometimes dream nasty things?'

Frank remains silent.

Teacher: 'Think it over. Think about all the things you've dreamed.'

Frank (after a long pause): 'I dreamed that a man was running after me, and I ran away and my heart beat hard.'

Teacher: 'So a man was running after you in your dream, was he! Oh well, it often happens that people dream silly things like that. Tell me, if you close your eyes, can you still see what the man looked like? What sort of a man was he?'

Frank: 'He was a little man.'

Teacher: 'Was he as big as you?'

Frank: 'No, he wasn't. He was smaller than me, much smaller.'

Teacher: 'Like a little man from Lilliput?'

Frank: 'Yes. Like that.'

Teacher: 'Do you often dream that someone is running after you?'

Frank: 'Oh, yes, often—robbers.'

Teacher: 'Robbers, eh? So there was more than one?'

Frank: 'Only two: a man and a girl.'

Teacher: 'And how big was the man?'

151

Frank: 'He was small, too. And I dreamed of a boy as well. He wanted to stab me.'

Teacher: 'So I suppose you wake up in the night and shout sometimes?'

Frank is silent.

Teacher: 'It sometimes happens that someone wakes up in the night and shouts if he's had a bad dream or if he's afraid. Only usually children don't know that they wake up in the night and scream. . . .'

Frank: 'I don't know it.'

Teacher: 'But your mother tells you about it the next day and asks you whether you were afraid again or whether you had a bad dream.'

Frank: 'Yes.'

Teacher: 'You like the day better, don't you? It isn't dark then . . . and you don't have such bad dreams. I can understand that. By the way, what do you do when you're at home during the day?'

Frank: 'Nothing.'

Teacher: 'Nothing! That's rather difficult to believe. What about your homework?'

Frank: 'Well, yes, homework.'

Teacher: 'Good. And what else?'

Frank: 'Reading.'

Teacher: 'Adventure stories, I suppose?"

Frank: 'Yes.'

Teacher: 'Stories like that are thrilling and exciting, aren't they?'

Frank: 'Yes.'

Teacher: 'Yes, of course they are. And what else do you do?'

Frank remains silent.

Teacher: 'Well, irritate your mother a little. . . . Squabble with your little sister. . . . Fight with your smaller brother, and so on?'

Frank: 'Oh, no!'

Teacher: 'No? What about fighting and squabbling with your brother? That's true enough, isn't it?'

Frank (grinning): 'Yes.'

Teacher: 'And you quarrel with your friends, too, don't you?'

Frank is again silent.

Teacher: 'You'd sooner be on your own?'

Frank: 'Yes.'

Teacher: 'And what about here in school?'

The Case of Frank

Frank is again silent.

Teacher: 'I've been told that you don't get on with your sums very well. I had that trouble, too, when I was your age. I didn't find it easy to understand what it was all about. Do you know what you'd like to be when you grow up?'

Frank makes no answer.

Teacher: 'A pastry-cook, perhaps?'

Frank laughs: 'No.'

Teacher: 'Well, what then?'

Frank shrugs his shoulders.

Teacher: 'Oh, so you haven't decided yet. Well, it doesn't matter much. There's time for you to think over quite a number of things still. For instance, how it comes about that you wake up in the night screaming . . . that you are afraid . . . that you are always squabbling with your brother . . . that things don't go as they might in school. Have you ever wondered why things were like that?'

Frank: 'No.'

Teacher: 'Shall I tell you how it all comes about?'

Frank says nothing but looks very astonished.

Teacher: 'I think you'll understand it when I explain it to you. . . . When you were born your elder sister was seven years old. Your mother was probably very happy when you arrived because now she had a boy to go with the girl. And your sister was already quite a big girl: she was even going to school. Your mother didn't have to do so many things for her as she had to do for you, the new baby. You couldn't walk, and you couldn't talk, and you couldn't tell people properly when anything was wrong. You were still very small and helpless and your mother had to feed you. She was always with you; she carried you around; she held you in her arms and sat you on her lap and was generally very kind and loving to you. You were the baby and so, of course, you had to have more attention.'

Frank: 'Like my sister now.'

Teacher: 'Yes, like your sister now. She's the baby and she's treated now as you were then. And I expect your mother says she's the baby sometimes?'

Frank: 'Yes.'

Teacher: 'There you are! And, you know, I don't think you are able to forget that you were once the baby and got most attention. That lasted for six years, and then your brother came along. After that, he was the baby and got most attention. And then you began to

153

think to yourself that your mother no longer loved you so much and that she loved your brother more. And perhaps you began to be angry with him because you thought he was taking your mother away. Perhaps you believe that still, do you?'

Frank: 'Oh, no!'

Teacher: 'During the day I'm sure you don't, because you know that it isn't a nice thing at all to be envious. But in the night? That's different, and what you really think comes out then. You still dream that there are robbers around trying to take things away from you. A little robber, you remember, and a little girl robber, too. Can't you really imagine who the little robber is who wants to take something away from you in your dream?'

Frank has opened his eyes wide and obviously at that moment a great light has dawned: 'My . . . my brother!'

Teacher: 'And once a little man ran after you. Do you recognize him, too?'

Frank: 'My brother!'

Teacher: 'And then on one occasion you thought: "What do we want a sister for?" You were certainly afraid that she was going to take something away from you, too. You see, when you have been the baby of the family for six years and believed all that time that you've got your mother all to yourself, and then someone else comes along, you start being afraid that they will take your mother's love away from you. I'm really not surprised at it, or that you think even now that your mother loves the others more than she loves you, that she hardly notices that you're there at all. And then, in order to impress it on her that you really are there, you've invented a wonderful trick without really thinking it out like that. It's a trick which doesn't let your mother forget that you're there. You start screaming in the night. Isn't that a wonderful way of showing your mother that she ought to pay more attention to you? Isn't it a wonderful way of showing your mother that she's neglecting you? Her own sleep is interrupted and she has to get up in the middle of the night and come and stroke your forehead and—just like she used to when you were still small, when you were still the baby of the family. . . . Do you know, I think you're beginning to understand why you have such dreams and why you wake up in the night screaming, and why you're always squabbling with your brother. You still think he's taking something away from you. Like a little robber! And you're not prepared to stand by and do nothing when you think you're

154

getting less than you ought to. There's a good deal of envy behind it, you know. But that's just the point: you didn't know it. Now you do know it. I'm not reproaching you for anything you've done up to now. You have just made a mistake and that can happen to anyone. But I think you can see your mistake now. If a mother pays more attention to a small child than she pays to an older one that doesn't mean that she loves the smaller child more. You mustn't lie in wait, jealously looking for every sign that the little ones get a little more love from their mother than you do. A mother's life is something like a wireless broadcast. There's one broadcasting station and many thousands of people listen in and they all hear the same. And if a few more people buy themselves wireless sets and listen in as well, they all hear just the same and nobody goes short although there's still only one broadcast. And it's just like that with a mother's love for her children. It isn't necessary for anyone to make all the fuss that you've been making, just in order to make it *look* as though your mother is giving you a bit more love than before. I think you can understand it all now. I repeat: I'm not making you any reproaches for what has happened up to now, and I'm not going to tell you what you ought to do from now on. I think from now on you'll act properly. . . .'

On December 12th the mother came to see me again, and this time her face was happy.

Mother: 'Mercy, what a relief! He hasn't woken up screaming in the night for a whole week. Every night I've kept awake listening and waiting, but everything has been calm and peaceful.'

Teacher: 'So there's been a very great change, has there?'

Mother: 'And what a change! I'm only afraid of its coming back again.'

Teacher: 'It is possible that it will start up again. But don't worry too much about it. Tell me exactly what has happened.'

Mother: 'I have written it down for you because I thought it would interest you.'

She hands over the following written report:

'Frank woke up screaming in the night from the 2nd to the 3rd. Bad dream: mother carried him off. In the night from the 4th to the 5th he talked in his sleep, but that was all, and not for more than a quarter of an hour perhaps: "It's true. . . . Perhaps he's right. . . . He's the only one who cares anything about me. . . . But that's only envy. . . ." In answer to a question, he made no reply and everything

155

was quiet. After a while the same thing happened. But since then nothing has happened at all.'

These few lines contained decisive information. In the night following my talk to him Frank woke up screaming again. According to the mother, he told her the next morning that he had dreamed that several men had seized her and carried her off. The mother found it strange that in telling her about this dream he had laughed—that had never happened before. In answer to her question as to why he was laughing, he replied that it was because he had had such a silly dream. Is it going too far to suppose that the boy laughed because for the first time he had understood the significance of the dream? That he had understood it within the framework provided by our first talk?

The second night passes without disturbance. During the third night he is disturbed and talks in his sleep—murmurs rather than talks, according to his mother. Only a few words here and there can be understood. What was he talking about? Obviously our conversation was in his mind. Ferdinand Birnbaum has pointed out that the decisive thing in education is the 'construction of the future perspective'. We discussed the matter very simply with Frank; in his own language, as far as possible. And yet he might easily have understood only our words and not their significance. But now his own words: 'It's true. . . .' confirm that he has not merely heard but understood. If he had been able to use our terminology then his agreement with what had been revealed to him would perhaps have been expressed in the words: 'It is quite true that my previous understanding of my relation to the community was false.'

But Frank goes on to say, 'Perhaps he's right. . . .' 'Perhaps' only. We can feel the resistance which Individual Psychology knows so well from its treatment of neurosis in adults. 'It's true. . . .' and, 'Perhaps he's right. . . .'—who can fail to appreciate the sudden confusion caused in the child's mind? Isn't it obvious enough that the child can feel the basis of his previous outlook on life slipping without having yet reached the really firm basis of a proper attitude towards the community? The child is in the grip of a violent crisis. Everything is at stake. The change of aim is about to take place. In this case we are witnesses of the mysterious process of change taking place in the creative ego.

'He's the only one who cares anything about me.' For Individual Psychologists this is a confirmation that the teacher has succeeded in establishing a warm and human contact with the child.

'But that's only envy. . . .' This fragment indicates that Frank has understood what is really behind it all. Of course, he can express in his own language only what lies within reach of his own thought. He cannot yet think objectively and say: 'Up to the present I have put my own ego instead of the community in the centre of my interests.' But he has, nevertheless, felt, experienced, understood—one can express it how one likes—that he has previously taken up a wrong attitude towards the community. The decisive thing is that we find him dealing unconsciously, in his sleep, with an impression he has received in his conscious state. We are quite deliberately using this terminology of the conscious and the unconscious here in order to illustrate something of decisive importance. In the case of Frank we can see a homogeneous personality bent to an aim: 'I want to live like the baby of the family!' And this formula is, so to speak, the motivating idea which builds the final house of the 'personality'. The 'personality' is the integration of its parts: its vitality, its tempo, its attitude, its failure, its memories, its attention, its dreams, its critical capacity, its degree of persistence, and so on. All these parts are fashioned in the relationship to the formal principle of the personality, to the constructive idea itself. Individual Psychology is in earnest when it adopts the principle of homogeneity, and its pedagogical activities are therefore directed not to the sympton, not to the fear, but to the personality which carries out the action itself, to the creative ego, and it seeks to persuade, even to provoke, precisely this creative ego to change direction and move towards the positive side of life.

But more than that: Individual Psychology does not divide an individual into the conscious and the unconscious; it speaks only of the 'unknown', and with this it means everything which lies beyond the sphere of conscious thought. The oneness of the personality is shown in the case of Frank by the fact that in a state of sleep he continued to work on a problem which had become clear to him in a state of wakefulness. It is no mystic 'it' that throws things and ideas into a wild and fantastic confusion inside us, but the uniquely existing 'ego', and it continues to work on in the dream at the colourful canvas of our psychological 'inwardness and outwardness', to use a phrase of W. Stern. Whether in sleep or wakefulness, the ego continues to perceive in a quite definite emotional direction; it recognizes false perspectives and it sets up new and positive aims. And thus, in the sense of Dr. Alfred Adler, the dream is a preparation for the practical task of living in a state of wakefulness. For Individual Psychology 'oneness' is a thesis of the life of the psyche which can be verified in observation. This verification is provided here by the utterances of Frank in his sleep, and therefore his case seems to me to be particularly interesting.

The mother informs us later that Frank still reads his 'shockers'. In our second talk with him we refer to them.

Teacher: 'Well, what are all your heroes doing now?'

Frank looks a little astonished. Incidentally, he now returns glance for glance and looks us straight in the eye.

Teacher: 'I mean the heroes of your shockers.'

Frank laughs.

Teacher: 'Read another good one, I suppose? They are heroes, aren't they? If one could onlybe a hero like that! Lots of children believe themselves to be the heroes when they read such stories. When they see themselves putting on a magic cap and doing all sorts of wonderful things they think they're big. But in reality they're still the same little boys and girls. And it's just the same with the bigger boys who think they're heroes when they read about them. Really they're running away from things. And they feel they are, too. And therefore they try to deceive themselves. I don't want a boy to be either a coward who's always afraid of everything or an imagined hero with a swelled head. I'm sure you agree with me.'

In the third talk with the mother we arrange for supplementary lessons to help Frank along with his sums because he is particularly backward in this subject. On account of the extra payment to the reliable teacher concerned the decision is not an easy one for the mother to take.

In our fourth talk on January 5th the mother brings the following written report:

'It was only on December 23rd that my son let me know what he wanted for Christmas: a motor-car that can be taken to pieces. He urged me to go out and buy it that very evening. Unfortunately, the shop was just putting up its shutters when we arrived. He was very disappointed and he grumbled a good deal and seemed afraid that our money would only be enough for the others and that he would get nothing. When we got home he sat in a corner with a black and discontented look. In the night from the 23rd to the 24th he got up, opened the door and wanted to walk in his sleep. Apparently he thought better of it and went back to bed instead, leaving the door wide open. He didn't scream as he used to, however, but he said several times in succession: "Tomorrow we'll see." On the 24th his grumbling about whether there would be enough for him began again. I bought him the motor-car although I had not reckoned with it. After Christmas, he saw the same motor-car in blue. His was red. At once he preferred the blue one and said: "That would have been much nicer. If only you had bought me that one!" Since then he has been sleeping peacefully. He's quite a good boy, but very irritable, and he pushes the two younger children around at the least provocation.'

Replying to a question, the mother said that he had suddenly stopped reading the 'shockers'.

From this report we can see that for a long time Frank had obviously suppressed his desires. His disappointment then threw him back into his former attitude. He got up in the night and wanted to wander off, something which he had never done before according to what he told his mother. But 'apparently' he thought better of it. There was no further screaming, although in such a situation one might have expected it. The revelation of the significance of the screaming had obviously touched him to the core. The change is in process but not yet complete, as can be seen from the information that he still pushes the younger children around at the slightest provocation.

We persuade the mother to allow him to invite two youngsters of his class to come home with him occasionally.

On January 26th the mother reports in writing:

'In the night from the 18th to the 19th January he slept badly and seemed to have a terrible dream, shouting: "They're coming! They're coming. . . It's all no use!" But he soon grew calm again. The next day he seemed very depressed. In the night from the 24th to the 25th his sleep was again disturbed, but he only talked. Once or twice he said: "But it isn't like that." The rest of what he said she could not understand. The next day he was in a good mood again. He was particularly pleased with a fountain-pen he was given. He even began to sing.'

Thus here we have the first real relapse. His words: 'They're coming. . . .' indicates a persecution or robbery dream. The words: 'It's all no use. . . .' seem to indicate that he is willing but doesn't think he can. Such a reaction is familiar to us. This also explains his depression the following day. About a week later he says: 'But it isn't like that!' And afterwards he is in a better mood again. I think the interpretation here is that the change in the essence of a personality is not the work of a moment or two. Perhaps I can make that clearer by a comparison. When Newton first consciously observed the fall of the famous apple he intuitively formulated the theory of gravity which he subsequently proceeded to develop patiently in all its ramifications. The process of change in a personality is probably something similar. The first sudden influx of light which reveals that a false aim has guided constructions has then to be worked out patiently in all its ramifications—a long process—and then thoroughly understood. The materialization of the constructional idea, namely the psychological expression, goes hand in hand with the understanding. With this we have touched on a problem which, in my view, has received too little attention, namely: how exactly does the process of change take place in a personality?

On January 26th the third talk took place with Frank.

Teacher: 'Have you been dreaming again at all?'

Frank: 'I dreamed that my brother had fallen into the Danube Canal and been drowned. I was so frightened that I ran off home.'

Teacher: 'How did you come to dream such a thing?'

Frank: 'I read something of the sort in the newspaper.'

Teacher: 'But many other people must have read the same thing and yet they didn't dream like that. No, I think the explanation is different. Now listen: if you thought: "If only my brother were dead!" you'd be shocked yourself at such an idea, wouldn't you? But if your brother falls into the water and is drowned, he is dead and you can think it without being shocked, because it isn't your fault. So the dream shows us that you want to get rid of your brother because you still don't like him. But he must be got rid of without your having to do anything about it. You still believe that he is the robber. But you have already seen that there's no point at all in a twelve-year-old boy still wanting to be the baby of the family. However, you forget that from time to time, and then you still want to be the baby.'

The school year rolls on. Now and again a few encouraging remarks are made. The auxiliary lessons meet with considerable difficulties because there are very big gaps to be filled and progress is slight. However, the mother no longer comes to the school, which suggests that the worst symptoms have disappeared. But on March 10th she comes again. Here is her written report:

The Case of Frank

'His sleep has been satisfactory. He has not screamed in the night for a long time. He also no longer throws himself around in bed so much when he ought to be fast asleep. On one occasion he did sit up in bed and whisper something, but I couldn't make out what it was. Afterwards he lay down again and slept on. He often complains of sleepless nights, but in reality he has always slept particularly well on the nights he complains of. In the mornings he is always in a good temper and whistles cheerfully. Formerly he was absolutely washed out and used to stand around with a black face. He has thus changed completely. And during the day he is quite happy. He even talks of the future. He often sings now. I follow his improvement with delight, but I am still afraid of a relapse.'

So Frank is only 'whispering' now. A very acceptable change of symptoms. Much more agreeable for his mother.

On March 31st his mother again reports in writing: 'Observation of my son during the past three weeks has had the following results: generally speaking he sleeps peacefully, but sometimes he sits up in bed, looks around and whispers something that I can't understand. I have noticed that some nights he lies awake for a long time in bed. During the day he is very cheerful. He often speaks of his future and about an apprenticeship, and he is looking forward to leaving school. He is very good to the younger children, but when he is in the least thwarted he gets very excited. He would do anything for his friends at school. His Easter present was not so big as that of the young children, but he did not complain and even seemed not to notice it. After his last arithmetic test he was rather put out, but he still hopes to pass.'

His hope was well founded; not because his work was now quite satisfactory but because the mathematics master was considerate enough to let things pass rather than impose any big strain on the general process of change which was going on in the boy. It was up to us now to deal with the change in the boy's symptoms.

Teacher: 'So the bigger nuisance is over now?'

As Frank looks blank the teacher explains: 'I mean the screaming at night. That doesn't happen any more, but instead you do other and less important things, though they have just the same sense: you lie awake, you sit up in bed, you look around, and sometimes you even do a bit of whispering. Well, if it gives you any pleasure. . . . It doesn't matter much. It doesn't disturb anyone. You needn't do it if you don't want to. But just as you like. However, as long as you do

L 161

do it, you and I know that you still have just a little longing to be the baby again. But, on the whole, we can be well satisfied with you. What nonsense I'm talking!—on the whole, *you* can be well satisfied with *yourself*. And that's wrong, too, isn't it? All I really mean is that now you are doing things properly. That's it. Just that and no more.'

At the end of the year his mother reported: 'He sleeps perfectly peacefully now. He doesn't even whisper any more in his sleep.'

Frank left school and started work as an apprentice. For a number of years his mother spoke of his doings with pride. Unfortunately, he was killed on the Russian front.

Envoi

In this book I have tried to indicate the wealth of educational opportunities open to teachers who have an understanding of Adler's Individual Psychology. My principal point has been that every child needs to be taught how to develop himself in relationship with other children and with the community at large. The community itself, if properly invoked, is itself a vital educational force enabling him to acquire this knowledge. It can sweep the child up and carry him along in the right direction, bringing out all his individual faculties while correcting a tendency to egocentricity. If he is a discouraged child, experiences of success are arranged for him. The class discussions begin to dissolve his inhibitions and the helper system works to compensate his inadequate training. In personal talks the teacher has the opportunity to reveal to the child the basic mistake in his attitude to life. The teacher can, as it were, switch the power of the community over to the individual or vice versa. Hour by hour, day by day, with endless devices to suit each child's needs, the teacher can gradually transform a backward or misdirected child into a happy and valuable member of society.

We accept, of course, that Education alone cannot abolish all the ills that flesh is heir to. Economic, political and social problems require for their solution trained economists, politicians and social workers. But to become a well-adjusted human being, conscious of his duties to the community as well as of his rights, also requires training.

An Individual Psychological teacher is, like any other teacher, part and parcel of the world of values. As a citizen he has to take his stand on religious, political, social and other issues. When he opens up this world of values to the child, he does so as an educator, but not distinctively as an Individual Psychological educator. His function as an Individual Psychological educator is to prevent the child from abusing the values he is shown by harnessing them to the service of his childish egotism.

We feel it necessary to make this distinction clear in order to prevent this book from being fatally misunderstood. Because we have not spoken a great deal about the education of the child to religious, aesthetic, economic, political and other such values this should not be taken to mean that Individual Psychology does not properly appreciate these values. On the contrary. It is only that Individual Psychology has no special lists of values to enumerate. As an educator, the Individual Psychologist has a relation to all these values. If, for instance, he is an American, then he will encourage the children in his charge to a warm love for and devotion to the United States; if he is an Englishman then he will stir their enthusiasm for England's greatness; if he is an Austrian then he will teach his children to love their own beautiful country. If he does these things, then, as an educator, he will be acting correctly. But he will not be acting specifically as an Individual Psychological educator.

Individual Psychology, therefore, claims no special knowledge in fields other than its own; it claims only to teach how to make the best use of all accepted knowledge. Most people would agree that it is a desirable thing to be a true artist, a sound economist or an honest politician; what perhaps is not always realized is that these ends are only attained by those who have first learned how to be a well-adjusted human being.

APPENDIX

The Austrian System of Education

The Austrian System of Education

In Austria attendance at school is compulsory. Children enter the so-called 'Volksschule' (Primary School) after they have become six years of age. In special cases, however, reception is dependent on the result of a test showing the fitness of these children. The children have to attend four classes of this Primary School. The attendance of the Primary School is compulsory for all children. Only on the grounds of a report by the district physician, children may have individual private tuition.

After finishing the Primary School, some of the pupils (between 25 per cent and 30 per cent) go to the so-called 'Mittelschule' (Secondary School) of which there are three types:

1. 'Humanistische Gymnasien' (Grammar Schools with Latin and Greek.)

2. 'Realgymnasien' (Grammar Schools with Latin and a living language), and

3. 'Realschulen' (Grammar Schools with two living languages, above all, English).

The rest of the children coming from the Primary School (70 per cent to 75 per cent), attend the so-called 'Hauptschule' (Central School, similar to the English Secondary Modern Schools), which in larger towns, has two streams. In the A-stream are more intelligent children, with a quicker way of working, greater readiness to learn, and interest in theoretical things. The B-stream is provided for children not so intelligent, with a slower way of working, interested more in manual things. Of course, it is possible that children of the B-stream transfer to the A-stream, if they improve; and vice versa.

Appendix

The attendance of the Central School as well as the attendance of the lower grade of some secondary schools, puts the children in the way of going:

(*a*) to the Higher grade of some Grammar School, or

(*b*) to some vocational school (Commercial School with lower standards or Commercial Secondary School with higher standards as a Preparatory School for the Mercantile Academy with university character, or some Technical School (textiles, chemistry, electrical engineering, etc.), or gives them

(*c*) the possibility (chosen by most of the children) to be apprenticed, which, however, is always connected with the attendance of the corresponding vocational school.

The attendance of the higher grade of a Grammar School ends with a final examination, which in the case of the 'Gymnasium' and 'Realgymnasium' entitles the child to enrol at one of the universities, whilst students of the 'Realschule' may go to a Polytechnic Institute. The study at a University ends with taking a doctor's degree (Dr. Med., D.D., M.A., LL.D.), while the study at a Polytechnic Institute ends with the degree of 'Diplom-Ingenieur' (engineer holding a technical high school diploma), which is equal to the doctor's degree of a University.

The Austrian schools are in general maintained and controlled by the State or the Individual Federal Province respectively. There are some private schools in existence (Roman Catholic and Protestant), but they, too, are State-controlled and must keep to the public syllabus.

It is worth mentioning that most schools in Austria have co-education. Only in larger places there are separate boys' classes and girls' classes. In Vienna about one-fourth of the Primary and Central Schools have co-education.

The children mentioned in my book, are *boys* of a Central School, between ten and fourteen years of age. Whether they belong to an A- or B-stream is not said. However, it is not essential.

Perhaps I should say a few words about the training of teachers.

1. Teachers for Primary Schools go to a Teachers' Training College for five years. They have to pass the Higher Certificate Examination (Matriculation). After two years of practical work as teachers, they have to pass a further examination and get the qualification to teach at Primary Schools. Only then can they be engaged definitely as Primary School teachers. For this examination, the teachers of

Vienna have to attend continuation courses at the Pedagogic
Institute of Vienna.

2. Teachers at Central Schools: To become a teacher at a Central
School, the Primary School teacher may attend training courses at
the Pedagogic Institute of Vienna, and specialize for a certain group
of subjects, e.g., German, geography, history or mathematics,
science, natural science, etc. After passing a special examination in
these subjects, he can become a definite Central School teacher.

3. Teachers at Secondary Schools must have eight terms at a
University and the examinations for certain subjects. Also the
training of teachers for Technical Schools takes place at a University.

Perhaps it should still be mentioned that the staffs of Primary and
Central Schools tend to include more and more women. In Vienna,
for instance, there are one-third men and two-thirds women.

Index

'Active' method (in education), 13, 45, 47

Adler, Dr. Alfred, 9, 11–14, 16, 24, 78, 120, 130, 157, 163

Alfred (case of), 45–7

Anticipation (as teacher's device), 31–2

Anxiety, 17

Arithmetic. *See* Mathematics

Arthur (case of), 121

Attention (desire for), 38, 138, 144 (paying), 25, 33, 40, 131–2, *see also* Inattention

Austro–Hungarian Empire, 11

Birnbaum, Ferdinand, 12, 27, 156

Brothers, 134–5, 149–54, 160

Burger, E., 55

Child Guidance Clinics, 11–15

Children's courts, 73 *et seq.*

Class discussions, 12, 34, 43, 47, Ch. III, 59, 66, 69–71, 79–83, 92, Ch. VII, 114, 132, 163

Class laws, 69 *et seq.*

Class organization, Ch. II, Ch. IV

Congress of Individual Psychology, 13

'Conscious', the, 157

Consistency (in education), 33

Co-operation, 16, 25, 47

Daydreams, 18

Democracy, 11–12

Delinquency. *See* Juvenile delinquency

Dethronement, 46

Discipline, 12–13, Ch. II, 47, 94

Discouragement, 28, 39–40, 76–8, 86, 93, 114, 131, 138–9, 163

Discussion. *See* Class discussions

Dreams, 17, 39, 41, 125–6, 128–9, 151–2, 154–61

Early memories, 125, 150–1, 157

Edgar (case of), 75

Edward (case of), 25

Education (systems, methods of), 10, 12–13, 22–4, 28–9, 42, 163, 166–8

Encouragement, 86–9

Eric (case of), 76–7

Exhortation, 25–6, 30

Experimental psychology, 23

Fascism, 14

Fathers, 37–8, 46, 121–4, 136

Fickert, Paul, 45

Forgetfulness, 37, 39, 43, 117, 119, 135

Frank (case of), Ch. XI

Free discussion. *See* Class discussions

Freud, S., 12

Ganz, Dr. M., 14

Glockel, 13

Grandmothers, 37–8, 41

Index

Group therapy, 12

Hapsburg Monarchy, 11, 13
Heckmann, Prof., 73
Helpers, helper system, 21, 42, 54, 92, 94–6, 99–100, 121, 128, 163

Identification (of teacher with pupils), 34–5, 81, 85, 117
Impatience, 42
Inattention, 25, 37, 42–3, *see also* Attention
Individual psychology, 9–10, 13–15, 27–9, 39–40, 44, 47, 55, 69–70, 74, 77–8, 83, 86–8, 92, 97, 130–1, 134–5, 138–9, 146–7, 156–8, 163–4
Individual Psychology, Congress of, 13
Experimental School, 13–14
Inferiority feeling, 119, 136
Introvert, 17
Irony, 32, 34, 61, 85

Jahn, E., 28
Jealousy, 46, 76
Juvenile delinquency, 11

Late-coming, 26, 74 *et seq.*, *see also* Truancy
Laws. *See* Class laws
Laziness, 26, 28, 37, 39, 77, 114, 119, 130–1
Leaders, 19, 21, 33, 35–6, 89–94, 98–100
Lefthandedness, 38–9, 116, 124
Life-Style, 27, 29, 35, 39–41, 47, 78, 93, 114, 119, 131, 135, 146
Loewy, Ida, 46
Lying, 37

Mann, Dr. Wilhelm, 73
Mathematics, 26, 37, 45, 133, 139, 143, 145, 149, 161
Memories. *See* Early memories
Monitors, 33, 63–4, 66, 69, 84–9

Mothers, 27, 37–8, 46, 76, 121, Ch. IX, 135–45, Ch. XI

Only child, 46

Pampering, 23, 46
Parents, 22–3, 25, 125, 131
'Possession' psychologies, 24
Problem children, 15, 27–8, 70, 78, Ch. VIII, 139
Punishment, 12, 20, 27–30, Ch. II, 60, 73–4, 77
Psychology, 11, *see also* Individual, Experimental, 'Possession'

Reininger, Karl, 22
Religion, 55, 164
Resistance (psychological), 69–71, 75, 100, 156
Rewards, 29–30
Rupert (case of), 35–44

School class, 12, 17 *et seq.*, 31 *et seq.*
School courts. *See* Children's courts
School inspectors, 22, 24
Secret associations, 104–13
Self-government (in schools), 63, Ch. V, 92, 96, 114
Sisters, 46–7, Ch. IX, 134–45, 148–54
Social Democracy (Austrian), 13
Spiel, Oskar, 12–15
St. Maday, Dr., 79
Stealing, 37, 39–40, 42–3
Stern, Dr. W., 157
Stupidity, 46, 130
Style of Life. *See* Life-Style
Success experiences, 30, 40–2, 77, 97, 121, 131, 163
Superiority striving, 29, 41
Symptoms, 26–8, 39–41, 76–7, 139, 147, 157, 160–1

'Taboo' sign, 62, 64

Talent, 23, 130–1, 145–6
Teachers (problems, tasks of), 9–10, 15–16, 22 *et seq.*, 44, 114 *et seq.*, 163–4
Tests, 23, 130
Theodore (case of), Ch. IX
Threats, 26–7, 30, 34, 60
Tidiness, 25, 74, *see also* Untidiness
Truancy, 24, 26, 28, 96, 118, *see also* Late-coming

'Unconscious', the, 157

Unpunctuality. *See* Truancy and Late-coming
Untidiness, 26

Vienna, 11, 13–15
Viennese Board of Education, 13
City Council, 13

Weekly Discussion Hour. *See* Class discussions
Willy (case of), Ch. X
World War I, 11
World War II, 14, 130